BEYOND
CIVILIZATION

Other Books by Daniel Quinn

Ishmael

My Ishmael: A Sequel

The Story of B

Providence: The Story of a Fifty-Year Vision Quest

BEYOND
CIVILIZATION

HUMANITY'S NEXT
GREAT ADVENTURE

DANIEL QUINN

What would happen if we
intentionally forged our social solutions
in the fires of creative chaos?

—JOHN BRIGGS AND F. DAVID PEAT

HARMONY BOOKS/NEW YORK

Grateful acknowledgment is made to the following: The Providence Journal Company for excerpts from "The Circus Atmosphere at Ninigret Park" (*Providence Journal-Bulletin,* July 12, 1994). Reprinted by permission. Anthony Weir for lines from *The Transcendental Hotel.* Reprinted by permission. Joseph Chassler for "LS of TP&D" from *Addict's Damn.* Reprinted by permission.

Published by Harmony Books, 201 East 50th Street, New York, New York 10022. Member of the Crown Publishing Group.

Random House, Inc. New York, Toronto, London, Sydney, Auckland

www.randomhouse.com

Harmony Books is a registered trademark and Harmony Books colophon is a trademark of Random House, Inc.

Printed in the United States of America

Library of Congress Cataloging-in-Publication Data

Quinn, Daniel.

Beyond civilization: humanity's next great adventure/Daniel Quinn.

1. Civilization—Philosophy. 2. Human ecology. 3. Social change.

4. Forecasting. I. Title.

CB19.Q56 1999

901—dc21   99-22636

ISBN 0-609-60490-2

10 9 8 7 6 5 4 3 2 1

First Edition

For Rennie

and for Hap Veerkamp and C.J. Harper,
with special thanks to the members of the 1998 Houston Seminar,
who played such a crucial role in the development of this book,
and to Scott Valentine and Sara Walsh in particular—
you kept us going and you kept me sane.

The homeless and the young are rapidly converging on the
socioeconomic territory I identify in this book as "beyond
civilization." The homeless have for the most part been thrust
into it involuntarily, while many of the young unknowingly
yearn for it, as anyone does who wants more from life than
just a chance to feed at the trough where the world is
being devoured. It is to them and their hopes that
this book is particularly dedicated.

PART ONE

Closing In on the Problem

I heard this, naturally, from my grandfather, he from his grandfather, he from his own grandfather, and so on, back many hundreds of years. That means this tale is very old. But it won't disappear, because I offer it to my children, and my children will tell it to their children, and so on.

GYPSY STORYTELLER LAZAROS HARISIADIS,

QUOTED BY DIANE TONG IN GYPSY FOLK TALES

A fable to start with

Once upon a time life evolved on a certain planet, bringing forth many different social organizations—packs, pods, flocks, troops, herds, and so on. One species whose members were unusually intelligent developed a unique social organization called a tribe. Tribalism worked well for them for millions of years, but there came a time when they decided to experiment with a new social organization (called civilization) that was hierarchal rather than tribal. Before long, those at the top of the hierarchy were living in great luxury, enjoying perfect leisure and having the best of everything. A larger class of people below them lived very well and had nothing to complain about. But the masses living at the bottom of the hierarchy didn't like it at all. They worked and lived like pack animals, struggling just to stay alive.

"This isn't working," the masses said. "The tribal way was better. We should return to that way." But the ruler of the hierarchy told them, "We've put that primitive life behind us forever. We can't go back to it."

"If we can't go back," the masses said, "then let's go forward—on to something different."

"That can't be done," the ruler said, "because nothing different is possible. Nothing can be *beyond* civilization. Civilization is a final, unsurpassable invention."

"But no invention is ever unsurpassable. The steam engine was surpassed by the gas engine. The radio was surpassed by television. The calculator was surpassed by the computer. Why should civilization be different?"

"I don't know *why* it's different," the ruler said, "It just *is*."

But the masses didn't believe this—and neither do I.

A Manual of Change

My first concept of this book was reflected in its original title: *The Manual of Change.* I thought of this because there's nothing the people of our culture want more than change. They desperately want to change themselves and the world around them. The reason isn't hard to find. They know something's wrong— wrong with themselves and wrong with the world.

In *Ishmael* and my other books, I gave people a new way of understanding what's gone wrong here. I had the rather naive idea this would be enough. Usually it *is* enough. If you know what's wrong with something—your car or your computer or your refrigerator or your television set—then the rest is relatively easy. I assumed it would be the same here, but of course it isn't. Over and over again, literally thousands of times, people have said to me or written to me, "I understand what you're saying—you've changed the way I see the world and our place in it—but what are we supposed to DO about it?"

I might have said, "Isn't it obvious?" But obviously it *isn't* obvious—or anything remotely like obvious.

In this book I hope to *make* it obvious.

Humanity's future is what's at stake.

Who are the people of "our culture"?

It's easy to pick out the people who belong to "our" culture. If you go somewhere—anywhere in the world—where the food is under lock and key, you'll know you're among people of our culture. They may differ wildly in relatively superficial matters—in the way they dress, in their marriage customs, in the holidays they observe, and so on. But when it comes to the most fundamental thing of all, getting the food they need to stay alive, they're all alike. In these places, the food is all *owned* by someone, and if you want some, you'll have to buy it. This is expected in these places; the people of our culture know no other way.

Making food a commodity to be owned was one of the great innovations of our culture. No other culture in history has ever put food under lock and key—and putting it there is the cornerstone of our economy, for if the food wasn't under lock and key, who would work?

What does "saving the world" mean?

When we talk about saving the world, what world are we talking about? Not the globe itself, obviously. But also not the biological world—the world of life. The world of life, strangely enough, is not in danger (though thousands and perhaps even millions of species are). Even at our worst and most destructive, we would be unable to render this planet lifeless. At present it's estimated that as many as two hundred species a day are becoming extinct, thanks to us. If we continue to kill off our neighbors at this rate, there will inevitably come a day when one of those two hundred species is our own.

Saving the world also can't mean preserving the world *as it is right now*. That may sound like a nice idea, but it's also out of reach. Even if the entire human race vanished tomorrow, the world wouldn't stay the way it is today. We will never, under any circumstances, be able to stop change on this planet.

But if saving the world doesn't mean saving the world of life or preserving it unchanged, what are we talking about? Saving the world can only mean one thing: saving the world *as a human habitat*. Accomplishing this will mean (*must* mean) saving the world as a habitat for as many other species as possible. We can *only* save the world as a human habitat if we stop our catastrophic onslaught on the community of life, for we depend on that community for our very lives.

Old minds with new programs

In my novel *The Story of B,* the middle volume of the trilogy that begins with *Ishmael* and ends with *My Ishmael,* I wrote, "If the world is saved, it will not be by old minds with new programs but by new minds with no programs at all." I'm afraid this is a case where the words are all easy, but the thoughts are slippery. I'll rephrase it. If we go on as we are, we're not going to be around for much longer—a few decades, a century at most. If we're still around a thousand years from now, it will be because we *stopped* going on as we are.

How will that have come about? How are we going to stop going on this way?

Here's how old minds think of stopping us. They think of stopping us the way they stopped poverty, the way they stopped drug abuse, the way they stopped crime. With programs. Programs are sticks planted in the mud of a river to impede its flow. The sticks *do* impede the flow. A little. But they never stop the flow, and they never turn the river aside.

This is why I can confidently predict that *if* the world is saved, it will not be because some old minds came up with some new programs. Programs never stop the things they're launched to stop. No program has ever stopped poverty, drug abuse, or crime, and no program ever *will* stop them.

And no program will ever stop us from devastating the world.

New minds with no programs

If the world is saved, it will not be by old minds with new programs but by new minds with no programs at all.

Why not new minds with new *programs?* Because where you find people working on programs, you don't find new minds, you find old ones. Programs and old minds go together like buggy whips and buggies.

The river I mentioned earlier is the river of vision. Our culture's river of vision is carrying us toward catastrophe. Sticks planted in the mud may impede the flow of the river, but we don't need to impede its flow, we need to divert it into an entirely new channel. If our culture's river of vision ever begins to carry us away from catastrophe and into a sustainable future, then programs will be superfluous. When the river's flowing where you want it to flow, you don't plant sticks to impede it.

Old minds think:	New minds think:
How do we stop these bad things from happening?	*How do we make things the way we want them to be?*

DANIEL QUINN

No programs at all?

Programs make it possible to look busy and purposeful while *failing*. If programs actually did the things people expect them to do, then human society would be heaven: our governments would work, our schools would work, our law enforcement systems would work, our justice systems would work, our penal systems would work, and so on.

When programs fail (as they invariably do), this is blamed on things like poor design, lack of funds and staff, bad management, and inadequate training. When programs fail, look for them to be replaced by new ones with improved design, increased funding and staff, superior management, and better training. When these new programs fail (as they invariably do), this is blamed on poor design, lack of funds and staff, bad management, and inadequate training.

This is why we spend more and more on our failures every year. Most people accept this willingly enough, because they know they're *getting* more every year: bigger budgets, more laws, more police, more prisons—more of everything that didn't work last year or the year before that or the year before that.

Old minds think:	New minds think:
If it didn't work last year, let's do MORE of it this year.	*If it didn't work last year, let's do something ELSE this year.*

If not programs, then what?

A man was found sitting in the middle of the desert in a contraption made of rocks, bits of lumber, and old, blown tires, which he was busily "steering" as if it were actually a vehicle in motion.

Asked what he was doing, the man said, "Driving home."

"You're never going to get there in this," he was told.

He said, "If not in this, then in what?"

We're like this man, busily trying to steer into the future in a Rube Goldberg assemblage of programs that has never taken us any farther than this man's pile of junk took him. Even after we've acknowledged that programs don't work and never have worked, however, it still somehow seems natural to ask, "If not programs, then what?"

I'd like to recast the question this way: "If programs don't work, then what *does* work?" In fact, I have an even better way of asking the question: "What works so well that programs are superfluous? What works so well that it never occurs to anyone to create programs to *make* it work?"

The answer to all these questions is: *vision.*

The invisibility of success

When things work, the forces that *make* them work are invisible. The universe at large is a notorious example of this. It took a towering genius to recognize the laws of motion and universal gravitation that now seem almost boringly obvious to us. Newton's genius was precisely the genius of seeing that which is so evident as to be unseeable. Every advance in science makes manifest a working that is cloaked by its very success.

The dancer's admonition is *Never let them see you sweat.* When it comes to the laws of the universe, this admonition becomes *Never let them see you at all: make them deduce your existence.* And indeed the laws of the universe are never directly observable, so we have no other way of discovering them except by deduction.

What works in the living community is similarly cloaked by its success. The basic laws of ecology have the beauty and simplicity of a fairy tale, but their existence only began to be suspected a century ago.

The invisibility of tribal success

People are fascinated to learn why a pride of lions works, why a troop of baboons works, or why a flock of geese works, but they often resist learning why a tribe of humans works. Tribal humans were successful on this planet for three million years before our agricultural revolution, and they're no less successful today wherever they manage to survive untouched, but many people of our culture don't want to hear about it. In fact, they'll vigorously deny it. If you explain to them why a herd of elephants works or why a hive of bees works, they have no problem. But if you try to explain why a tribe of humans works, they accuse you of "idealizing" them. From the point of view of ethology or evolutionary biology, however, the success of humans in tribes is no more an idealization than the success of bison in herds or whales in pods.

Our cultural excuse for failure is that humans are just "naturally" flawed—greedy, selfish, short-sighted, violent, and so on, which means *anything* you do with them will fail. In order to validate that excuse, people *want* tribalism to be a failure. For this reason, to people who want to uphold our cultural mythology, any suggestion that tribalism was successful is perceived as a threat.

Making tribal success visible is the work of my other books and will not be repeated here.

Conspicuous success, invisible source

Our culture has been conspicuously successful, in the sense that it has overrun the world. For most of our history, this success was perceived as merely an inevitability, the working out of human destiny. People no more wondered about it than they wondered about gravity. When Europeans "discovered" the New World, they considered it a sacred duty to take it over. The people who were already living there were just in the way, like trees or rocks or wild animals. They had no real business being there, as we did. For us to take over this hemisphere was just part of the larger plan (presumably God's plan) for us to take over the entire world.

That we were *able* to overrun this hemisphere (and indeed the entire world) came as no surprise to us. This is simply what was *meant* to be, so naturally it *came* to be. No one is amazed when clouds produce rain.

Before Newton, people didn't wonder why unsupported objects are compelled to fall to the ground. They just figured, what else *could* they do? They *have* to fall to the ground, and that's that. Our historians have always been in the same condition when it comes to our tremendous cultural success. They don't wonder why we were compelled to take over the world. They just figure, what else *could* we have done? We *had* to take over the world, and that's that.

Vision is like gravity

Vision is to culture what gravity is to matter. When you see a ball roll off a table and fall to the floor, you should think, "Gravity is at work here." When you see a culture make its appearance and spread outward in all directions until it takes over the entire world, you should think, "Vision is at work here."

When you see a small group of people begin behaving in a special way that subsequently spreads across an entire continent, you should think, "Vision is at work here." If I tell you that the small group I have in mind were followers of a first-century preacher named Paul and that the continent was Europe, you'll know the vision was Christianity.

Dozens or perhaps even hundreds of books have investigated the reasons for Christianity's success, but not one of them was written before the nineteenth century. Before the nineteenth century it seemed to everyone that Christianity no more needed reasons to succeed than gravity does. It was bound to succeed. Its success was sponsored by destiny.

For exactly the same reason, no one has ever written a book investigating the reasons for the success of the Industrial Revolution. It's perfectly obvious to us that the Industrial Revolution was bound to succeed. It could no more have failed than a ball rolling off a table could fall toward the ceiling.

That's the power of vision.

The spread of vision

Every vision is self-spreading, but not every vision spreads itself in the same way. In a sense, the spreading mechanism *is* the vision.

Our culture's spreading mechanism was population expansion: *Grow, then get more land, increase food production, and grow some more.* Christianity's spreading mechanism was conversion: *Accept Jesus, then get others to accept him.* The Industrial Revolution's spreading mechanism was improvement: *Improve on something, then put it out there for others to improve on.*

Clearly all spreading mechanisms have one thing in common: they confer benefits on those who do the spreading. Those who get more land, increase food production, and grow are rewarded with riches and power. Those who accept Jesus and get others to accept him are rewarded with heaven. Those who improve on something and put it out there for others to improve on are rewarded with respect, fame, and wealth. The benefit conferred shouldn't, however, be confused with the mechanism itself. Our culture wasn't spread by people becoming rich and powerful, Christianity wasn't spread by people going to heaven, and the Industrial Revolution wasn't spread by people winning respect, fame, and wealth.

Vision: success without programs

When a chemist puts water in a test tube and adds salt, an angel comes along and dissolves the salt into charged particles called ions. Because we perceive the universe to be self-governing according to internally consistent and comprehensible principles, the angel in this story seems completely superfluous to us. We therefore cut it away with Occam's razor.

Although historians now look for the reasons behind Christianity's success, they aren't looking for programs. Christianity thrived in the Roman world because the people of that time were ready for it, and historians would no more expect to find programs at work there "promoting" Christianity than chemists would expect to find angels at work in their test tubes. (It might be argued that Constantine's Edict of Milan, allowing Christians freedom of worship, was a program of support, but in fact it merely permitted what two and a half centuries of persecution had been unable to stop, much as the twenty-first amendment to the U.S. Constitution merely permitted what fourteen years of Prohibition had been unable to stop.)

In the same way, the spread of our culture has never had to be kept going by any program. It has never flagged for a single instant, and the same can be said of the Industrial Revolution.

When the vision turns ugly

When the river of vision begins to carry people in a direction they don't like, they start planting sticks to impede its flow. These are the sticks I call programs.

Most programs take this form: *Outlaw the thing that's bothering you, catch people who do it, and put them in jail.*

Old minds think:	New minds think:
We have to write tougher and more comprehensive laws.	*No unwanted behavior has ever been eliminated by passing a law against it.*

The fact that programs of this sort invariably fail doesn't trouble most people.

Old minds think:	New minds think:
If it didn't work last year, let's do MORE of it this year.	*If it didn't work last year, let's do something ELSE this year.*

Every year, without fail, we outlaw more things, catch more people doing them, and put more of them in jail. The outlawed behavior never goes away, because, directly or indirectly, it's supported by the strong, invisible, unrelenting force called vision. This explains why police officers are much more likely to take up crime than criminals are to take up law enforcement. It's called "going with the flow."

Programs aren't wicked, just inadequate

When someone has received life-threatening injuries in a car accident, the medics in the ambulance do whatever they can to keep him alive till they reach a hospital. This first aid is essential but ultimately inadequate, as everyone knows. If there's no hospital at the end of the road, the patient will die, because the ambulance just doesn't have the resources a hospital does.

The same is true of programs. There are many programs in place today that are staving off our death—programs to protect the environment from becoming even more degraded than it is. Like the first aid in the ambulance, these programs are essential but ultimately inadequate. They're ultimately inadequate because they're essentially reactive. Like the medics in the ambulance, they can't make good things happen, they only make bad things less bad. They don't bring into being something good, they only drag their feet against something bad.

If there's no hospital at the end of the road, the patient in the ambulance will die, because first aid (useful as it is) just doesn't have the capacity to keep him alive indefinitely. If there's no new vision for us at the end of the road, then we too are going to die, because programs (useful as they are) just don't have the capacity to keep us alive indefinitely.

But how could we get along without programs?

Once, in the land of broken legs, the inhabitants heard rumors of another land far away where people moved around freely, because no one's legs were broken. They scoffed at these tales, saying, "How could anyone get around without crutches?"

To say that the Industrial Revolution is a terrific example of what people can do without programs is an understatement. It's a mind-boggling example. From the time Giambattista della Porta dreamed up the first "modern" steam engine nearly four hundred years ago to the present, this vast, world-transforming movement has been carried forward by vision alone: *Improve on something, then put it out there for others to improve on.* Not a single program was ever needed to forward the Industrial Revolution. Rather it was forwarded by the confident realization in millions of minds that even a small new idea, even a modest innovation or improvement over some previous invention could improve their lives almost beyond imagination. Over a few brief centuries, millions of ordinary citizens, acting almost entirely from motives of self-interest, have transformed the human world by broadcasting ideas and discoveries and furthering these ideas and discoveries by taking them step by step to new ideas and discoveries. To acknowledge all this is not to make the Industrial Revolution a blessed event—but neither does condemning it as a catastrophe make it less than the greatest outpouring of creativity in human history.

But how will we live then?

No paradigm is ever able to imagine the next one. It's almost impossible for one paradigm to imagine that there will even *be* a next one. The people of the Middle Ages didn't think of themselves as being in the "middle" of anything at all. As far as they were concerned, the way they were living was the way people would be living till the end of time. Even if you'd managed to persuade them that a new era was just around the corner, they would've been unable to tell you a single thing about it—and in particular they wouldn't have been able to tell you what was going to make it *new*. If they'd been able to describe the Renaissance in the fourteenth century, it would have *been* the Renaissance.

We're no different. For all our blather of new paradigms and emerging paradigms, it's an unassailable assumption among us that our distant descendants will be just exactly like us. Their gadgets, fashions, music, and so on, will surely be different, but we're confident that their mindset will be identical—because we can imagine no other mindset for people to have. But in fact, if we actually manage to survive here, it will be because we've moved into a new era as different from ours as the Renaissance was from the Middle Ages—and as unimaginable to us as the Renaissance was to the Middle Ages.

How can we achieve a vision we can't imagine?

We can do it the way it's always done: *one meme at a time.* I'm aware this statement needs explaining. The best would be for you to read Richard Dawkins's *The Selfish Gene,* but in case this isn't convenient for you right this second, I'll summarize. Briefly, *memes are to cultures what genes are to bodies.*

Your body is a collection of cells. Every cell in your body contains a complete set of all your genes, which Dawkins likens to a set of building plans for a human body—and your body in particular. At conception, you were a single cell—a single set of the building plans for your body, one half of the set received from your mother and the other half received from your father. This one cell subsequently divided into two cells, each containing the complete set of building plans for your body. These two subsequently divided into four, the four into eight, the eight into sixteen, and so on—each containing the complete set of building plans for your body.

A culture is also a collection of cells, which are individual humans. You (and each of your parents and all your siblings and friends) contain a complete set of memes, which are the conceptual building plans for our culture. Dawkins coined the word *meme* (rhymes with *theme*) to apply to what he perceived to be the cultural equivalent of the gene.

The leaping of genes and memes

Dawkins suggests that memes replicate themselves in the "meme pool" (the thing I call culture) in a way that is analogous to the way genes replicate themselves in the gene pool. That is, they leap from mind to mind the way genes leap from body to body. Genes leap from body to body by way of reproduction. Memes leap from mind to mind by way of communication: in lullabies heard in the cradle, in fairy tales, in parents' table conversation, in jokes, in television cartoons, in the funnies, in sermons, in gossip, in lectures, in textbooks, in movies, in novels, in newspapers, in song lyrics, in advertisements, and so on.

A great deal of ink (real and virtual) has been spilled over Dawkins's memes. Some authorities have dismissed them as nonexistent or as nonsense. Others have gone so far as to wonder if memes exist in brains in as physical a sense as dendrites or glia cells. I leave them to it.

Every culture is a collection of individuals, and each individual has in his or her head a complete set of values, concepts, rules, and preferences that, taken together, constitute the building plans for that particular culture. Whether you call them memes or marglefarbs is irrelevant. There can be no question whatever that they exist.

Small percentages, big differences

Unless you happen to be a geneticist, you'll probably be surprised to learn that we differ from chimpanzees by only a very small percentage of genes. We expect it to be the other way around. We're so manifestly different from chimpanzees that we expect there to be a vast genetic gulf between us. Obviously the genes we *don't* share must in some way "make all the difference." But it would be a mistake to think that, without these genes, humans would be chimpanzees—or that, with these genes, chimpanzees would be humans. Humans aren't just chimpanzees with extra genes, nor are chimpanzees just humans with missing genes. Nothing in the world of genetics (or any other world, for that matter) is ever that simple.

Only a very small percentage of memes differentiated the Renaissance from the Middle Ages, but obviously the new ones "made all the difference." The authority of the Church waned, new humanist ideals emerged, the development of the printing press gave people new ideas about what they could know and think about, and so on. To produce the Renaissance, it wasn't necessary to change out ninety percent of the memes of the Middle Ages—or eighty or sixty or thirty or even twenty. And the new memes didn't have to come into play all at once. Indeed, they *couldn't* have come into play all at once. The Renaissance was ready for Andrea del Verrocchio long before it was ready for Martin Luther.

Which memes do we need to change?

This question is a lot easier to answer than might be expected. The memes we need to change are the *lethal* ones.

Richard Dawkins puts it with irreducible simplicity: "A lethal gene is one that kills its possessor." It may well strike you as unfair and somehow unreasonable for such things as lethal genes even to exist. You may also wonder how lethal genes manage to remain in the gene pool at all. If they kill their possessors, why aren't they eliminated? The answer is that genes don't all come into play at the same time. Most genes, obviously, begin work during the fetal stage, when the body is being built. Some, just as obviously, are dormant until the onset of adolescence. Lethal genes that come into play before adolescence are of course quickly eliminated from the gene pool, because their possessors are unable to pass them on by reproduction. Lethal genes that come into play early in adolescence also tend to be eliminated, but those that come into play in middle or old age remain in the gene pool, because their possessors are almost always able to pass them on through reproduction before succumbing to their lethal effect.

Lethal memes

A lethal meme is one that kills its possessor. For example, the Heaven's Gate cultists possessed a lethal meme that made suicide irresistibly attractive to them—but I'm not much interested in memes that are lethal to individuals. I'm interested in memes that are lethal to cultures (and to our culture in particular).

Lethal genes don't start out as benign and then later become lethal. Rather, they start out as having no effect or another effect, which only later becomes lethal. The same is true of lethal memes. Early Semitic witnesses to our cultural beginnings saw that their neighbors had plucked some memes from the gods' own tree of wisdom. They said, "Our neighbors to the north have got the idea they should rule the world. This meme is benign in the gods but deadly in humans." Their prediction was accurate, but it didn't come true immediately. The memes that made us the rulers of the world are lethal, but they didn't have a lethal effect ten thousand years ago—or five thousand or two thousand. They were at work, turning us into the *rulers* of the world, but their deadliness didn't become evident until this century, when they began turning us into the *devastators* of the world.

Ridding ourselves of those memes is a matter of life and death, but it *can* be done. I know this because it *has* been done—by others. Many times.

PART TWO ※

Closing In on the Process

. . . was defaced and abandoned . . .

. . . the city's ultimate collapse . . .

Whatever happened . . .

. . . the city was destroyed . . .

The collapse may have been caused by . . .

. . . sites were abandoned . . .

. . . towns were abandoned . . .

PAST WORLDS: THE TIMES ATLAS OF ARCHAEOLOGY

Survival machines for genes

Each of us is a mixture of genes received from our mother and father, and of course our mother and father are mixtures of genes received from their mothers and fathers. Knowing this, we tend to think of our genes as things that keep us going, generation after generation. But here's a picture that's closer to reality: If genes could think, they would think of *us* as what keeps *them* going, generation after generation.

I say this is closer to reality because in fact we don't survive as individuals, but our genes do. You and I, like all other living creatures, are temporary mobile homes for the genes we received from our parents, and our job (from our genes' point of view) is to make sure we give those genes a home in the next generation—in our children, of course. As far as our genes are concerned, when an individual unit of temporary housing has no more reproductive value, it's ready for recycling. This should show you clearly enough what's what around here. We tend to think of ourselves as the VIPs of the earth, the bosses and big shots, but in fact we're just the disposable vehicles in which our genes are riding to immortality. "Survival machines for genes" is the name Richard Dawkins gives these disposable vehicles.

Survival machines for memes

In the same way, we're the disposable vehicles in which our memes are riding to immortality. These memes come to us from all the speakers who are vocal wherever we happen to grow up—parents, siblings, friends, neighbors, teachers, preachers, bosses, co-workers, and everyone involved in producing things like textbooks, novels, comic books, movies, television shows, newspapers, magazines, internet sites, and so on. All these people are constantly repeating to each other (and of course their children, their students, their employees, and so on) the memes they've received during their lifetime. All these voices taken together constitute the voice of Mother Culture.

In case it needs saying, the immortality I'm talking about here isn't absolute. Our genes will not survive the death of our planet, a few billion years hence, and our memes have a much shorter life expectancy than that.

The fidelity of copying

Let's say you've created a one-page document on your computer and printed it out. If you make a xerographic copy of this original on a good machine, you'll have a hard time telling the original from the copy, which we'll call A. But if you use A to make another copy, B, and then use B to make C and then use C to make D and then use D to make E, this last copy will be easily distinguishable from the original. This makes it evident that a little bit of the original was lost in each copying generation. Between one generation and the next, no loss is visible to the naked eye, but a build-up of losses is clearly visible between the original and copy E. This happens because you used an analog copier.

But if you go back to the document in your computer and copy what's on the screen as file A, then copy file A as file B, then copy file B as file C, and so on, you could go on making copies of this document all day, one after another, and at the end of the day it's very likely that no difference would be detectable between the original and the very last copy. This happens because you used a digital copier rather than an analog copier. This fidelity of copying is the very foundation of the digital revolution.

Genetic and memetic replication

Genes replicate themselves with the same sort of astounding fidelity—but the same can't be said of memes unless we add some qualifications. Among tribal peoples living undisturbed (as, for example, in the New World before the European incursion), the transmission of memes from generation to generation generally takes place with virtually perfect fidelity. This is why they perceive themselves to have been living this way "from the beginning of time." To us, therefore, tribal cultures seem static (a word that carries for us a whiff of the pejorative) in comparison with our own culture, which seems dynamic (a word that carries for us a whiff of the admirable).

Our culture is dynamic (as we perceive it) because our memes are often very volatile: newborn in one generation, swaggering with power in the next, doddering in the next, and laughably old-fashioned in the next. Nonetheless, there is a central core of culturally fundamental memes that we've been transmitting with total fidelity from the foundation of our culture ten thousand years ago to the present moment. Identifying this core of fundamental memes isn't very difficult, and it would have been done long ago if someone had thought of it.

The best way to live

One of these fundamental memes is *Growing all your own food is the best way to live*. Apart from a few anthropologists (who know perfectly well that this is a matter of opinion), this meme goes unchallenged in our culture. And when I say that a few anthropologists know this is a matter of opinion, I mean they know it chiefly as a professional obligation. As anthropologists, they know that the Bushmen of Africa wouldn't agree that growing all your food is the best way to live, nor would the Yanomami of Brazil or the Alawa of Australia or the Gebusi of New Guinea. As individuals, however, these anthropologists would almost universally consider this to be the best way to live and would unhesitatingly choose it for themselves above all others. Outside this profession, it would be hard to find *anyone* in our culture who doesn't subscribe to the belief that deriving all your food from agriculture is the best way to live.

It's impossible to doubt that this meme entered our culture at the very moment of its birth. We wouldn't have become full-time farmers unless we believed it was the best way to live. On the contrary, it's self-evident that we began to grow all our food for precisely the same reason we *still* grow all our food—because we were convinced this was the best way to live.

Or . . .

Maybe they just sort of fell into it?

It's tempting to imagine that agriculture represents the path of least resistance for people trying to make a living, but in fact nothing could be further from the truth. Growing your own food represents the path of *greatest* resistance, and the more of it you grow, the greater the resistance. It's been established beyond a shadow of a doubt that there is an exact correlation between how hard you have to work to stay alive and how great your dependence on agriculture is. Those who grow the least also work the least, and those who grow the most also work the most. The amount of energy it takes to put three ounces of corn in a can of water on your supermarket shelf is almost beyond belief, as is the amount of time you must work in order to possess those three ounces of corn.

No, the founders of our culture didn't just fall into a lifestyle of total dependence on agriculture, they had to whip themselves into it, and the whip they used was this meme: *Growing all your own food is the best way to live.*

Nothing less could imaginably have done this amazing trick.

Maybe they were just hungry?

A hunter-gatherer who needs 2,000 calories a day to live has to expend only 400 calories to get them, because that's the rate at which hunting and gathering pays off—1 calorie of work gets you 5 calories of food. By contrast, a farmer who needs 2,000 calories a day to live has to expend 1,000 calories to get them, because that's the rate at which farming pays off—1 calorie of work gets you 2 calories of food.

For a food-hungry person to trade hunting-gathering for farming is like a money-hungry person trading a job that pays five dollars an hour for one that pays two dollars an hour. It makes utterly no sense, and the hungrier you are, the less sense it makes.

Farming is less efficient at banishing hunger than hunting and gathering, but it unquestionably confers other benefits (most notably, providing a base for settlement and eventually civilization), and it was to secure these benefits that the founders of our culture ultimately adopted a lifestyle of total dependence on agriculture. From that point, it became a matter of complete conviction among us that growing all your food is the best way to live. We had invested in that meme and in the future would protect that investment at any cost.

New World adopters of the meme

We weren't the only people in ancient times to recognize the benefits of growing all our food. Among the notable adopters of this meme in the New World were the Maya, the Olmec, the people of Teotihuacán, the Hohokam, the Anasazi, the Aztecs, and the Inca.

What's significant for our study of this most fundamental meme is that, by the time Europeans arrived in the New World at the end of the fifteenth century, only the latest of these civilizations, the Aztec and the Incan, were still clinging to it.

The Maya

The Maya probably became full-time agriculturalists not long after we did, but (like us) they didn't begin to look like civilization-builders for several thousand years. Their first great cities in Yucatán began to emerge around 2000 B.C.E., coincident with the founding of the Middle Kingdom of Egypt and actually ahead of the founding of Babylonia by some two centuries.

The Maya flourished for nearly three thousand years. Then at the beginning of the ninth century of the common era, the cities of the south suddenly began to be abandoned and before long were left standing empty. The cities of the north continued to flourish for a time under the domination of the Toltec but collapsed when the Toltec themselves collapsed in the thirteenth century. Mayapán, to the west, then emerged as the last great stronghold of Maya civilization, but this remnant was itself only another two centuries away from collapse.

This is, by design, the sort of account you'd find in an ordinary encyclopedia or historical atlas. Although it begins by talking about people, it immediately becomes the tale of something else, something like a vast ocean liner steaming through time. It carries passengers, to be sure, but these are mere ballast, necessary only in the sense that without them the ship must immediately go bottom-up and sink.

The Olmec and Teotihuacán

The Olmec agriculturalists of coastal Veracruz and Tabasco built great ceremonial centers, principally at San Lorenzo and La Venta. San Lorenzo, the oldest, flourished from 1200 B.C.E. to 900 B.C.E., when (as it's said) it "was defaced and abandoned." The very same thing happened at La Venta five centuries later. Lesser sites continued to be occupied for a time, but the destruction of La Venta marked the end of Olmec dominance in the area.

Some two hundred years later one of the great cities of the ancient world began to be built in central Mexico. Teotihuacán was destined to become the world's sixth largest city by 500 C.E. For two hundred and fifty years it flourished as the center of its own empire, then abruptly the usual happened. It "was destroyed"—burned and perhaps even "ritually" wiped out. The ruins were occupied for a time, but the city was dead.

The Hohokam and the Anasazi

The people who occupied the desert lands of southern Arizona from about the time of Christ strike us as being hard workers rather than civilization-builders. Their memorable undertakings, beginning around 700 C.E., were not cities but vast networks of irrigation ditches that enabled them to grow all their own food. Single ditches, as much as 25 feet wide and 15 deep, could extend as far as 16 miles, and one network along the Salt River connected 150 miles of ditches. The work began to be abandoned at the beginning of the fifteenth century, and within decades the workers became the Hohokam—"Those Who Vanished," in the language of the Pima Indians of the area.

The Anasazi occupied the Four Corners region, where modern-day Arizona, New Mexico, Utah, and Colorado meet. They flourished only briefly, beginning around 900 C.E., and built no great cities, but achieved a striking lifestyle in small towns and high-rise cliff dwellings. It was all abandoned soon after 1300.

Looking for the actors

In writing these capsule histories, I've followed the popular model for such accounts, starting in the active voice, with people *doing* things, and ending in the passive voice, with things *being done*—to "sites" or "cities" or "civilizations." The end always comes when sites are "abandoned," "destroyed," "defaced," "burned," or "desecrated"—one never learns by whom. One is left with a vague impression of mystery, as if these things had happened in the Bermuda Triangle or the Twilight Zone.

The authors of these accounts are clearly uneasy with the truth, which is that these civilizations were all destroyed and abandoned by the very people who built them. The Maya walked away from their cities under their own steam—they weren't whisked away in flying saucers. The Olmec themselves defaced and abandoned San Lorenzo and La Venta, and Teotihuacán was torched by its own citizens. One day the ditch-tenders of southern Arizona downed tools and walked away, and on another day the villagers and cliff-dwellers of Chaco Canyon and Mesa Verde did the same.

All these peoples did something even more outrageous that is almost never alluded to in accounts of this kind. It was bad enough that they abandoned their civilizations, but what they did next is almost unthinkable: *they stopped farming*. They stopped growing all their own food.

They gave up the very best way of living there is.

"Those Who Vanished"

In a very real sense, they all deserve to be called Hohokam, these strange peoples who slipped out of their magnificent robes, put aside the tools they'd used to create immortal works of art, trashed their plans for temples and pyramids, discarded literacy, mathematics, and the most advanced calendars in the world, consigned to oblivion elaborate state religions and whole political systems . . . and melted away into whatever landscape was at hand—tropical jungles, lush plains, or high deserts. Of course, none of them actually vanished. They just took up less conspicuous ways of making a living, either by foraging or by some mixture of foraging and farming.

But any way you cut it, they deliberately threw over what *we* think to be the very best lifestyle in the world for something inferior. They knew what they were doing, and they did it anyway . . . again and again and again. Naturally there are explanations. Inexplicable behavior can't be allowed to *remain* inexplicable. Anthropologist Jeremy A. Sabloff notes that dozens of hypotheses have been put forward to explain the Mayan collapse, "including overuse of the soil, earthquakes, hurricanes, climatic changes, diseases, insect pests, peasant revolts, and invasions," and the Maya are no exception. The same and other hypotheses have been advanced to explain all the other collapses. They all have something in common, as Professor Sabloff neatly concludes: "None of these explanations has proved to be totally satisfactory."

Why none will EVER be satisfactory

No such explanation will ever be satisfactory, because we all know these things:

- The soil may be depleted *here,* but it's not depleted *everywhere.*
- Earthquakes and hurricanes don't last forever.
- Climatic changes can be ridden out.
- Diseases run their course.
- Insect pests come and go.
- Peasant revolts can be put down—or survived.
- Invaders can be repelled—or absorbed.

It couldn't have been things like this that made these people quit, because look at *us.* These things are mere inconveniences compared to what *we've* faced—all these things, plus much worse: famines, wars of every kind, inquisitions, government by torture and assassination, endlessly rising crime, corruption, tyranny, madness, revolution, genocide, racism, social injustice, mass poverty, poisoned water, polluted air, two devastating world wars, and the prospect of nuclear holocaust, biological warfare, and extinction. We faced all that and more—and never once have been tempted to abandon our civilization.

There *had* to be something else at work—or missing—among these people. And indeed there *was* something else.

What a difference a _____ makes!

Two guys on an airplane. One falls out, then a moment later so does the other. The first guy splatters on the ground like a ripe tomato. The second lands on his feet and walks away. It's obvious that the second had something the first didn't, and what he had is also obvious: a parachute.

Two guys face a gunman. One takes a bullet in the chest and falls dead. The other takes a bullet in the chest, then calmly fires back, shooting the gunman dead. Again it's obvious that the second one had something the first didn't, and what he had is also obvious: body armor.

Two civilizations. One goes along for a while, then maybe something bad happens (or maybe not) and suddenly everyone just walks away from it. The other civilization goes along for much longer, constantly suffering every conceivable catastrophe—but no one dreams of walking away from it for even one second.

Again it's obvious that the second civilization had something the first didn't—but exactly *what* it had is not so obvious.

It had a meme.

For want of a meme, a civilization was lost

One can imagine how desperately the pontiffs, potentates, dynasts, princes, pendragons, princelings, rajahs, hierophants, priests, priestesses, and palace guards of all these tottering civilizations must have desired to implant in the minds of their vacillating subjects this very simple concept: *Civilization must continue at ANY cost and must not be abandoned under ANY circumstance.*

It goes without saying, however, that implanting alone isn't enough. To take effect, a meme must be accepted without question. You can't talk people into accepting an absurd idea like this one on the spur of the moment. They have to hear it from birth. It has to come to them from every direction and be buried in every communication, the way it is with us.

All these peoples started out believing that the best way to live is by growing all your own food. Why else would they become full-time farmers? They started out that way and went on that way for a long time. But then some very predictable things began to happen. For example, the Maya, the Olmec, and the people of Teotihuacán became rigidly stratified into wealthy, all-powerful elites and impoverished, powerless masses, who naturally did all the grunt work that made these civilizations magnificent. The masses *will* put up with this miserable life— we know that!—but they inevitably begin to get restless. We know that too.

When the underclass becomes restless

Our history is full of underclass insurrections, revolts, rebellions, riots, and revolutions, but not a single one has ever ended with people just *walking away*. This is because our citizens *know* that civilization must continue at any cost and not be abandoned under any circumstance. So they *will* go berserk, *will* destroy everything in sight, *will* slaughter all the elite they can get their hands on, *will* burn, rape, and pillage—but they will never just *walk away*.

This is why the behavior of the Maya, the Olmec, and the rest is so unfathomably mysterious to our historians. For them, it seems *self-evident* that civilization must continue at any cost and never be abandoned under any circumstance. How, then, could the Maya, the Olmec, and the others *not* have known it?

But this is exactly what was missing in the minds of these peoples. When they no longer liked what they were building, they were *able* to walk away from it, because they *didn't* have the idea that it must continue at any cost and not be abandoned under any circumstance.

This meme makes the same difference between them and us as the parachute makes between the two guys falling from the plane or the body armor makes between the two guys facing the gunman.

What about all the others?

There's no evidence that the Hohokam and the Anasazi had become divided into all-powerful upperclasses and powerless underclasses. But there is some evidence that the Hohokam were leaning in that direction. Platform mounds in the Mesoamerican style (built *by* whom if not an emerging underclass?) were beginning to show up here and there, as were leisure-class ball courts (built *for* whom if not an emerging upperclass?). The Anasazi experiment was the briefest of all the ones I've examined here and the least highly developed as a civilization (if it merits that name at all). Regardless, the same is true for all. When, for whatever reason, they no longer liked what they were building, they were *able* to walk away from it, because they didn't have the idea that it must continue at any cost and not be abandoned under any circumstance.

I've mentioned (but not discussed) the other two great civilizations of the New World, the Incan and the Aztec. Their early and middle development followed lines laid down by the Maya and Olmec, but their ending was not in their own hands, since they were destroyed by invading Spanish armies in the sixteenth century. Obviously it's impossible to know how they might have gone on if left to their own devices, but my guess is that (lacking that critical meme) they would ultimately have followed the example of all the others.

The Cultural Fallacy

To us, the meme *Civilization must continue at any cost and not be abandoned under any circumstance* seems intrinsic to the human mind—self-evident, like *The shortest distance between two points is a straight line*. A mind that doesn't possess that meme hardly seems human to us.

We imagine humanity was *born* with this meme in its head. *Homo habilis* knew he should be civilized but didn't have the brains to do it. *Homo erectus* knew he should be civilized but didn't have the skills to do it. *Homo sapiens* knew he should be civilized but couldn't figure out what it takes. *Homo sapiens sapiens* knew he should be civilized, had the brains and the skills to do it, and got down to it as soon as he figured out that agriculture is what it takes. Naturally he knew it must continue at any cost and not be abandoned under any circumstance.

What, therefore, was *wrong* with all these New World civilization-builders? It's hard for us to get over the idea that there was something very mysterious about them. They knew (because it's self-evident) that civilization must not be abandoned under any circumstance—but they abandoned it anyway.

This is an example of the Cultural Fallacy, which is: *The memes of our culture arise from the very structure of the human mind itself, and if you don't have them, there must be something wrong with you.*

Naturally this too is a meme.

The other mystery of "Lost Civilizations"

The first mystery of the New World civilization-builders is easy to discern, because it manifests itself as something they *did:* they destroyed what they built. The second mystery is less easy to discern, because it only manifests itself as something they *didn't* do: they didn't overrun the world.

At the height of their development, the Maya occupied an area no larger than Arizona. By the time we reached the same height of development, we occupied all the Middle East and Europe and much of India and Southeast Asia. There was no one around equipped to oppose a Mayan advance north or south of their homeland in Yucatán and Guatemala, had they chosen to make it. They might have civilized the entire hemisphere in the thousands of years they had—had they chosen to do it. Oddly, mysteriously, they didn't choose to do it.

The Olmec were content to occupy a homeland smaller than Connecticut, and had the metropolis Teotihuacán been built in the center of Los Angeles, its imperial reach would have fallen well short of the city limits.

What was wrong with these people? What did they lack that we had?

Go ahead, guess.

The missing meme

Unlike the soldiers who preceded them, the settlers of the New World didn't come dragging their national borders behind them. Rather, they came dragging a common *cultural* border behind them. Behind this border, people from Europe, the Near East, and the Far East could settle down comfortably side by side, because they were cultural siblings. Whether they came from England, China, Turkey, Russia, Ireland, Egypt, Thailand, or Denmark, they were vastly more like each other than they were like the savages on the other side of that border. (And, naturally, they didn't go slave hunting except on the other side of that border.)

This wasn't special to the New World. It was this way from the beginning. The border that rippled outward in all directions from the Fertile Crescent wasn't a national border, it was a cultural one. It wasn't soldiers who conquered the Old World, it was farmers, who taught their neighbors, who taught their neighbors, who taught their neighbors, taking the message outward in a circle ever-widening until it enclosed all but the undiscovered New World on the other side of the planet.

The meme we brought with us to the New World was nothing new. We'd been spreading it from the beginning: *Ours is the one RIGHT way for people to live and everyone should live like us.* Possessing this meme, we made ourselves cultural missionaries to the world, and, lacking this meme, the Maya, the Olmec, and the others did not.

Holy work

When Columbus set off westward across the Atlantic, he wasn't looking for an empty continent to colonize, he was looking for a trade route to the Orient. And if he'd actually bumped into Asia instead of America, the people of Europe would have said to themselves, "Let's go do some business with these Orientals." No one would have dreamed of saying, "Let's go over there, drive off the Orientals, and take Asia for ourselves."

But of course Columbus didn't bump into Asia, he bumped into America, which, as he saw it, was unoccupied (aside from a few savages). When the people of Europe heard this, they didn't say to themselves, "Let's go do some business with those savages." They said to themselves, "Let's go over there, drive off the savages, and take America for ourselves." This wasn't rapacity but rather sacred duty. When a farmer clears a field and puts it to the plow, he doesn't think of himself as taking that field away from all the wildlife that makes its home there. He isn't stealing it, he's putting it to the use God intended from the beginning. Before being cultivated, this land was merely going to waste. And that's how the settlers saw the New World. The natives were letting it all go to waste, and by taking it away from them and putting it to the plow, they were performing holy work.

The New World fell not to a sword but to a meme.

Pyramid builders

The worker hordes who built the pyramids of Mesoamerica were not more miserable than the ones who built the pyramids of Egypt. The workers of Mesoamerica merely perceived themselves as having an alternative to misery, which they eventually exercised (by walking away). We didn't, so we slogged on, building a ziggurat here, a Great Wall there, a bastille here, a Maginot Line there—and on and on and on—to the present moment, when our pyramids are not being built at Giza or Saqqara but rather at Exxon and Du Pont and Coca Cola and Proctor & Gamble and McDonald's.

I visit many classrooms, and the students one way or another always bring me round to a point where I ask how many of them are champing at the bit to get out there and start working on the pyramids their parents worked on throughout their lives and their parents before them. The question makes them uneasy, because they know they're *supposed* to be absolutely thrilled at the prospect of going out there to flip burgers and pump gas and stock shelves in the real world. Everyone's told them they're the luckiest kids on earth—parents, teachers, textbooks—and they feel disloyal not waving their hands at me. But they don't.

Pharaohs

It took Khufu twenty-three years to build his Great Pyramid at Giza, where some eleven hundred stone blocks, each weighing about two and a half tons, had to be quarried, moved, and set in place *every day* during the annual building season, roughly four months long. Few commentators on these facts can resist noting that this achievement is an amazing testimonial to the pharaoh's iron control over the workers of Egypt. I submit, on the contrary, that pharaoh Khufu needed to exercise no more control over his workers at Giza than pharaoh Bill Gates exercises over his workers at Microsoft. I submit that Egyptian workers, relatively speaking, got as much out of building Khufu's pyramid as Microsoft workers will get out of building Bill Gates's pyramid (which will surely dwarf Khufu's a hundred times over, though it will not, of course, be built of stone).

No special control is needed to make people into pyramid builders—if they see themselves as having no choice but to build pyramids. They'll build whatever they're told to build, whether it's pyramids, parking garages, or computer programs.

Karl Marx recognized that workers without a choice are workers in chains. But his idea of breaking chains was for us to depose the pharaohs and then build the pyramids *for ourselves,* as if building pyramids is something we just can't stop doing, we love it so much.

The Mayan Solution

The meme is as strong today among us as it was among the stone-draggers of ancient Egypt: *Civilization must continue at any cost and not be abandoned under any circumstance.* We're making the world uninhabitable to our own species and rushing headlong toward extinction, but *Civilization must continue at any cost and not be abandoned under any circumstance.*

This meme wasn't lethal to pharaonic Egypt or to Han China or to medieval Europe, but it's lethal to us. It's literally us or that meme. One of us has to go—and soon.

But . . .

But . . .

But . . . *But surely, Mr. Quinn, you're not suggesting we go back to living in caves and catching dinner on the end of a spear?*

I've never suggested such a thing or come anywhere close to suggesting such a thing. Given the realities of our situation, going back to the hunting-gathering life is as silly an idea as sprouting wings and flying off to heaven. We can walk away from the pyramid, but we can't melt away into the jungle. The Mayan solution is utterly gone for us, for the simple reason that the jungle itself is gone and there are six billion of us. Forget about *going back.* There is no back. Back is gone.

But we can still walk away from the pyramid.

Beyond the pyramid

If, having walked away from the pyramid, we can't melt into the jungle, what on earth *can* we do? Here's how the gorilla sage of *Ishmael* answered that question: "You pride yourselves on being inventive, don't you? Well, invent." Not surprisingly, his pupil shrugged this off as a nonanswer—and I'm sure most readers did the same. They did this because in our meme about civilization there's another meme that is implicit: *Civilization is humanity's ULTIMATE invention and can never be surpassed.* That's precisely *why* it must be carried forward at any cost, because there cannot possibly be any invention beyond it. If we were to abandon civilization (gulp!), then we'd be *finished!*

If there's going to be any future for us, our first invention must be a meme-killer. We must destroy in ourselves and in the people around us the meme proclaiming civilization to be an unsurpassable invention. It is, after all, *just* a meme—just a notion peculiar to our culture. It isn't a law of physics, it's just something we've been taught to believe that our parents were taught to believe—as were their parents and their parents and their parents and their parents all the way back to Giza and Ur and Mohenjo-Daro and Knossos and beyond.

Since there's no better meme-killer than another meme, try this one on for size:

Something BETTER than civilization is waiting for us.

Something *much* better—unless you're one of those rare individuals who just *loves* dragging stones.

PART THREE

Walking Away from the Pyramid

I went out to buy transcendence
and came back with a telephone.
ANTHONY WEIR

I am twenty-two years old and I will wait no longer.
SCOTT VALENTINE

Social organization and natural selection

No one is surprised to learn that bees are organized in a way that works for them or that wolves are organized in a way that works for them or that whales are organized in a way that works for them. Most people understand in a general way that the social organization of any given species evolved in the same way as other features of the species. Unworkable organizations were eliminated in exactly the same way that unworkable physical traits were eliminated—by the process known as natural selection.

But there is an odd and unexamined prejudice against the idea that the very same process shaped the social organization of *Homo* over the three or four million years of his evolution. No one is surprised to learn that the shape of a claw or a pattern of coloration has come down to the present because it works for the possessor of that claw or pattern of coloration, but many are reluctant to entertain the idea that any human social organization could have come down to the present for the same reason.

Definitions and examples

Lifestyle (or way of life): A way of making a living for a group or individual. Hunting and gathering is a lifestyle. Growing all your own food is a lifestyle. Scavenging (for example, among vultures) is a lifestyle. Foraging (for example, among gorillas) is a lifestyle.

Social organization: A cooperative structure that helps a group implement its way of life. Termite colonies are organized into a three-caste hierarchy consisting of reproductives (king and queen), workers, and soldiers. Human hunter-gatherers are organized into tribes.

Culture: The totality of what is communicated by one generation of a people to another by means of language and example. The Yanomami of Brazil and the Bushmen of Africa have a common lifestyle (hunting and gathering) and a common social organization (tribalism) but not a common culture (except in a very general sense).

The mysterious persistence

Our cultural vision was shaped by people who were perfectly satisfied with the notion that the universe they saw was in its final form, and had come into being in that form—in a single stroke, so to speak. The Genesis tale of creation didn't originate this notion, it merely affirmed it: God did his work, saw it was in no need of improvement, and that was that.

It hasn't been easy for us to give up this notion, and in fact many people unconsciously cling to it even while talking the talk of evolution. This is why the disappearance of New World civilizations seems mysterious to our historians. If their world-view were fundamentally Darwinian instead of fundamentally Aristotelian, they'd realize that what they're seeing in these disappearances is merely natural selection at work, and the aura of mystery would vanish.

During our three or four million years on this planet it can hardly be doubted that thousands of cultural experiments have been made among humans. The successes have survived—and the failures have disappeared, for the simple reason that eventually there was no one around who wanted to perpetuate them. People will (ordinarily) put up with being miserable for only so long. It's not the quitters who are extraordinary and mysterious, it's we, who have somehow managed to persuade ourselves that we must persist in our misery whatever the cost and not abandon it even in the face of calamity.

Some DO want more than adequacy

Before becoming full-time farmers, the Maya, the Olmec, and all the rest practiced hunting and gathering or some combination of farming and foraging. *Doesn't the fact that they eventually became full-time farmers indicate they were less than perfectly satisfied with these lifestyles?* That's exactly what it indicates.

At some point the idea of making all their living from agriculture seemed more attractive than the traditional way. This doesn't necessarily mean they hated their previous life, but it certainly means they judged the agricultural life to be more promising. Very probably they didn't regard their venture into the agricultural life as an experiment at all but as a permanent, irrevocable choice. If so, this doesn't negate the role of natural selection in this process but rather underscores it. Each of these peoples began by abandoning a traditional lifestyle for an innovation that seemed to promise more of what they wanted. When the innovation ended up giving them less of what they wanted, they abandoned it to resume their previous way of living. The innovation in each case had failed the test.

But doesn't this indicate that their traditional lifestyles were less than perfect? Certainly it does. Natural selection is a process that separates the workable from the unworkable, not the perfect from the imperfect. Nothing evolution brings forth is perfect, it's just damnably hard to improve upon.

Tribalism the workable

As I've said, if you note that hive life works well for bees, that troop life works well for baboons, or that pack life works well for wolves, you won't be challenged, but if you note that tribal life works well for humans, don't be surprised if you're attacked with an almost hysterical ferocity. Your attackers will never berate you for what you've said but rather for things they've *invented* for you to say, for example, that tribal life is "perfect" or "idyllic" or "noble" or simply "wonderful." It doesn't matter that you haven't said any of these things; they'll be as indignant as if you had.

Tribal life is not in fact perfect, idyllic, noble, or wonderful, but wherever it's found intact, it's found to be working well—as well as the life of lizards, racoons, geese, or beetles—with the result that the members of the tribe are not generally enraged, rebellious, desperate, stressed-out borderline psychotics being torn apart by crime, hatred, and violence. What anthropologists find is that tribal peoples, far from being nobler, sweeter, or wiser than us, are as capable as we are of being mean, unkind, short-sighted, selfish, insensitive, stubborn, and short-tempered. The tribal life doesn't turn people into saints; it enables ordinary people to make a living together with a minimum of stress year after year, generation after generation.

What would you expect?

After three or four million years of human evolution, what would you expect but a social organization that works? How else could *Homo habilis* have survived, except in a social organization that worked? How else could *Homo erectus* have survived, except in a social organization that worked? And if natural selection provided *Homo habilis* and *Homo erectus* with workable social organizations, why would it fail to provide *Homo sapiens* with one? Humans may have tried many other social organizations in those three or four million years, but if so, *none of them survived.* In fact, we *know* that humans have tried other social organizations.

The Maya tried one—and found after three thousand years that it didn't work (at least not as well as tribalism). *They returned to tribalism.*

The Olmec tried one—and found after three hundred years that it didn't work (at least not as well as tribalism). *They returned to tribalism.*

The people of Teotihuacán tried one—and found after five hundred years that it didn't work (at least not as well as tribalism). *They returned to tribalism.*

The Hohokam tried one—and found after a thousand years that it didn't work (at least not as well as tribalism). *They returned to tribalism.*

The Anasazi tried one—and found after four hundred years that it didn't work (at least not as well as tribalism). *They returned to tribalism.*

Not one of their experiments survived—but tribalism did. And that's what natural selection is all about.

If you like it so much . . .

People who dislike what I'm saying will challenge me this way: "If you're so crazy about the tribal life, why don't you get a spear and go live in a cave?"

The tribal life isn't about spears and caves or about hunting and gathering. Hunting and gathering is a lifestyle, an occupation, a way of making a living. A tribe isn't a particular occupation; it's a social organization that facilitates making a living.

Where they're still allowed to, gypsies live in tribes, but they're obviously not hunter-gatherers.

Similarly, circus people live in tribes—but again, obviously, they're not hunter-gatherers. Until recent decades there were many forms of traveling shows that were tribal in organization—theatrical troupes, carnivals, and so on.

What people like about tribal societies

Tribes exist for their members—and for all their members, because all are perceived as involved in the success of the tribe. When the tent goes up, there's no one in the circus more important than the construction crew. When the rigging goes up, there's no one more important than the riggers. When the show begins, there's no one more important than the performers, human and animal. And so it goes, through every phase of circus life.

Among hunter-gatherers, success obviously has nothing to do with money. In the circus, of course, everyone knows the show must make money in order to continue, but it's the circus, not the money, that provides the livelihood. I mean that they don't keep the circus going in order to make money; they make money in order to keep the circus going. (An artist might see it this way: there's a difference between painting in order to make money and making money in order to paint.)

The tribe is what provides them with what they need, and if the tribe is gone, they're all out of luck. Everyone wants the circus owner to make money, because if he stops making money, the show will close. Everyone's interest lies in the success of the whole. What's good for the tribe is good for everyone, from the owner down to the cotton-candy butchers.

I lean on the example of the circus to emphasize the fact that the tribal life isn't something that just worked long ago or just for hunter-gatherers.

Is there really such a thing as "the circus"?

If there's such a thing as "the theater," "the opera," and "the movies," then why wouldn't there be such a thing as "the circus"? But is it really tribal?

It's because the circus is tribal that we notice when a particular circus ceases to be tribal. The history of the Ringling Bros. and Barnum & Bailey Circus is unmistakably a history of circus tribes, but by now that particular circus is just a big business, as hierarchical as General Motors or United Airlines. No one mistakes a show like the Ice Capades for a tribal affair; it began as big business and has never been anything else.

Many small businesses start in a very tribal way, with a few partners pouring in all their resources and taking out only what's needed to survive, but this tribal character quickly disappears if the company becomes a conventional hierarchy. Even if it develops tribally, with new members extending the living to include themselves, it risks losing its tribal character if it becomes too large. At a certain size it must either stop growing or begin to organize itself as a tribe of tribes, which is probably the best way to understand the kinds of circuses you're likely to see in any big city today.

A tribe is a coalition of people working together as equals to make a living. A tribe of tribes is a coalition of tribes working together as equals to make a living; each tribe has a boss, as does the coalition as a whole.

Circus people are tribal people

What a tribal people transmits to the next generation is not a ready-made fortune but rather a reliable way to make a living. For this reason, the Busch family of brewers is a clan but not a tribe. What the current generation of Busches received from the previous generation was not a way to make a living but a ready-made fortune that will be passed on to the next generation.

By contrast, the world-famous circus performers known as the Great Wallendas have no billion-dollar corporation to transmit to succeeding generations. What they have to transmit is a way to make a living. The living isn't ready-made for them (as it was for August Busch III, who wouldn't have to work a day in his life if he didn't want to). Just as each succeeding generation of hunter-gatherers receives from the preceding the knowledge and practice of hunting and gathering (but must ultimately do their own hunting and gathering to stay alive), each succeeding generation of Wallendas receives from the preceding the knowledge and practice of circus performance (but must ultimately do their own performing to stay alive).

In an ethnic tribe, it's not at all uncommon to see three and even four generations at work side by side. The same thing is seen in circus tribes like the Wallendas, where no one is amazed if twelve-year-old Aurelia Wallenda performs the Cloud Swing with a forty-seven-year-old uncle, Alexandre Sacha Pavlata, a sixth-generation circus performer.

"I beg to differ!"

Just as many will see the aptness of classifying the circus as a tribe, others will rise up to denounce it as false or absurdly idealized. It will be pointed out, for example, that circuses routinely hire casual laborers who work for a day or a week and then are gone. These day-laborers are rarely members of the tribe and rarely become members of the tribe—all perfectly true (though it doesn't change the fact that some *do* become members of the tribe).

In very small circuses, all the work is done by the same group of people, who set up the equipment, man the booths, perform, and work with the animals. In larger circuses, however, bosses, performers, and workers are seen as belonging to different social classes, which theoretically (at least in some circuses) don't fraternize. I have to wonder, however, about the validity of seeing these as "social classes." It's possible, in an ordinary social setting, to imagine the worker class dreaming of overthrowing the "ruling" class. But this would be nonsense in a circus setting. What imaginable good would it do circus performers to "overthrow" the bosses? What imaginable good would it do circus workers to "overthrow" the performers? Rather than saddle the circus with "social classes" that don't quite work, I feel it makes better sense to think of the circus as a tribe of tribes, much as, for example, the Sioux were a tribe of tribes.

Tribal tales

One July day in 1986, reporter Ron Grossman of the *Chicago Tribune* traveled with "the last little mud show in America" as it departed New Windsor, Illinois, and set up at Wataga, thirty miles away. This was the Culpepper and Merriweather Great Combined Circus touring company, consisting of six performers, one roustabout, three goats, six dogs, as many Shetland ponies, and two young tag-alongs in the great tradition of Toby Tyler. While helping stake down the circus's fifty-by-seventy-foot tent in Wataga's Firemen's Park, owner and ringmaster Red Johnson recalled his own circus history, which began at age nine.

"My mother woke me real early one morning and we went to watch the Cole Bros. Circus set up. I remember really flipping for the blacksmith's shop," he said while swinging an eighteen-pound sledgehammer in alternating strokes with clown B.J. Herbert and tightrope walker Jim Zajack. "Afterwards, she got me a souvenir circus book and on the inside cover wrote: 'Don't get any ideas.'"

"Funny thing is my folks said the same thing when they gave me a circus book one Christmas," Zajack said. But by age seventeen, he'd worn them down enough to let him take what was supposedly a summer job with the Franzen Bros. Circus. He never went back home again, except when a show folded.

"The circus," he told Grossman, "is like a little tribe of nomads. Once initiated, you don't drop out."

D A N I E L   Q U I N N

"Here you're part of something."

Terrell "Cap" Jacobs, a whip-cracker with Culpepper and Merriweather, zeroed in on the hierarchical nature of the bigger circuses, noting that they have "the same kind of pecking order" as society in general. "On Ringling's, performers think it's beneath them to talk to roustabouts. Everybody has his own job to do; and, after the performance, everybody goes back to the private world of his own RV. Here, we're a family. We all work together, perform together, eat together, and, yes, bitch and moan at each other. There's not enough of us to play chiefs and Indians. It's got to be a democracy."

But it isn't just tiny shows that experience this tribal democracy. In 1992 David LeBlanc, tent boss (and later operations manager) for Big Apple Circus, said: "You have a total community here. I grew up in the suburbs, and I couldn't tell you the name of the people who live next to my parents, and I lived there for fifteen years. Here you not only live in the neighborhood, you're also working together for a common goal. You're part of something."

After helping a female member of the crew uproot a particularly stubborn tent stake, LeBlanc said, "That's the circus attitude. She has the heart. And you know what? That had nothing to do with her job. She was just helping out. People here are willing to do anything. In the real world, people demand a ten-minute break after working three hours, but here people are just devoted to what they do."

The turn away from tribalism

People don't plant crops because it's less work, they plant crops because they want to settle down and live in one place. An area that is only foraged doesn't yield enough human food to sustain a permanent settlement. To build a village, you must grow some crops—and this is what most aboriginal villagers grow: some crops. They don't grow all their food. They don't need to.

Once you begin turning all the land around you into cropland, you begin to generate enormous food surpluses, which have to be protected from the elements and from other creatures—including other people. Ultimately they have to be locked up. Though it surely isn't recognized at the time, locking up the food spells the end of tribalism and beginning of the hierarchical life we call civilization.

As soon as the storehouse appears, someone must step forward to guard it, and this custodian needs assistants, who depend on him entirely, since they no longer earn a living as farmers. In a single stroke, a figure of power appears on the scene to control the community's wealth, surrounded by a cadre of loyal vassals, ready to evolve into a ruling class of royals and nobles.

This doesn't happen among part-time farmers or among hunter-gatherers (who have no surpluses to lock up). It happens only among people who derive their entire living from agriculture—people like the Maya, the Olmec, the Hohokam, and so on.

D A N I E L   Q U I N N

From tribalism to hierarchalism

Every civilization that enters history *ex nihilo* (that is, from no previous civilization) enters with the same basic hierarchal social organization firmly in place, whether it emerges in Mesopotamia, Egypt, India, China, or the New World. How this remarkable result came about (doubtless through some process of natural selection) would make an interesting study—but not my study. *Why* it happened I leave to others. *That* it happened is undisputed.

The rough outlines of this social organization are familiar to everyone through the Egyptian model. You have a highly centralized state organization that consolidates in itself all economic, military, political, and religious power. The ruling caste, headed by a living deity in the shape of a pharaoh, Inca, or other divine monarch, is supported by a priestly bureaucracy that regulates and supervises the labor force conscripted for (among other things) the construction of palace and ceremonial complexes, temples, and pyramids.

The tribe is of course long gone—has by this time been gone for centuries, if not millennia.

What folks dislike about hierarchies

To be fair, I suppose I might divide this into two sections: What the rulers *like* about hierarchal societies and What everyone else *doesn't* like about them, but I doubt if anyone really needs me to explicate the first of these.

What people (aside from rulers) don't like about hierarchal societies is that they don't exist for all their members in the same way. They provide a life of unbelievable luxury and ease for the rulers and a life of poverty and toil for everyone else. The way rulers benefit from the success of the society is vastly different from the way the masses benefit, and the pyramids and the temples testify to the importance of the rulers, not to the masses who build them. And so it goes, through every phase of life in a hierarchal society.

The difference between the circus and Disney World is that the circus is a tribe and Disney World is a hierarchy. Disney World has employees, not members. It doesn't provide these employees with a living, it just pays them wages. The employees are working for themselves, and if Disney World can no longer pay them, they'll abandon it immediately. The owners have an investment in its success and benefit from its success. The employees are just employees.

Kids of all ages run off to join the circus. No one runs off to join Disney World.

But aren't tribes actually hierarchal?

This is a question asked by people who hate the idea that the tribal life actually works for people. The answer is, no, this is not what's found. Tribes have leaders, to be sure, and sometimes very strong leaders, but leadership carries little or nothing in the way of special benefits that are denied to other members of the tribe. Has there never arisen a tribe that has "gone hierarchal," where the leader has made himself into a despot? I'm absolutely certain this has happened, perhaps thousands of times. What's important to note is that no such tribe has *survived*. The reason isn't hard to find—people don't *like* living under despots. Again, that's natural selection at work: tribes ruled by despots fail to hold onto their members and become extinct.

In the circus everyone wants there to be a boss, taking care of business, making sure the circus stays in the black, making unpleasant decisions about who's going to be hired and fired, settling disputes, working out contracts, and dealing with local authorities. Without a boss, the circus would disappear in a hurry, but the boss is just another person with a job—the job of being boss. The boss isn't envied or even particularly admired. The stars of the show get the glory (as well as the highest salaries and the fanciest clothes), but they're nothing remotely like a ruling class.

Dreaming away the hierarchy

The ruled masses of our culture have been no less miserable than the ruled masses of the Maya, the Olmec, and other civilization-quitters we've examined. The difference between us and them is that we possess (or are possessed by) a complex of memes that so far have utterly barred us from quitting. We're absolutely convinced that civilization cannot be surpassed by any means and so must be carried forward even at the price of our own extinction.

Unable to walk away, we've used three very different rationales to make sense of our inaction.

The first rationale: justifying it

One reason we tend to think of East and West as culturally distinct is that Easterners have a different way of rationalizing the hierarchy under which they live; as they see it, this hierarchy results from the fundamental operation of the universe, which assures the realization of karma by means of reincarnation. Under the theory of karma, one's sins and virtues are punished or rewarded in this and subsequent lives. Thus if you're born to the life of an untouchable in Bhaktapur, India, where you can never hope to rise to any occupation above cleaning latrines, you have no one to blame but yourself. You have no grounds to envy or hate the Brahmans who shun and despise you; their life of felicity and leisure is only what they deserve, just as your life of poverty and misery is only what you deserve.

In this way the arrangement of people into high, middle, and low classes is shown to be justice made manifest in a divinely ordered universe. If I'm rich and well fed and you're poor and starving, this is only as it should be.

Buddhism may be seen as offering relief from this rigid posture of resignation to one's lot.

The second rationale: transcending it

Buddha and Jesus alike assured their listeners that the poor and downtrodden are (or ultimately will be) better off than the rich and powerful, who will find it almost impossible to attain salvation. The poor can live most happily, Buddha said, possessing nothing and living on joy alone, like the radiant gods. The meek (that is, the ones who always end up building the pyramids) will inherit the earth, Jesus said, and the kingdom of God will turn the hierarchy upside down; the kingdom of God will belong to the poor, not to the rich, and rulers and ruled will change places, making the first last and the last first. Jesus and Buddha agree that, contrary to appearances, riches don't make people happy. Rather, says Buddha, riches just make them greedy. And the poor shouldn't envy the rich their treasures, which are always subject to being stolen by thieves or eaten up by moths and rust; rather, Jesus says, they should accumulate incorruptible treasures in heaven.

These are the "consolations" that led Karl Marx to call religion "the opium of the people." This opium carries the masses out of their misery and up into the empyrean of tranquil acceptance. More important, from the viewpoint of the ruling class, this opium keeps them quiet and submissive, the promised inheritance of the meek remaining firmly and forever *in the future.*

The third rationale: overthrowing it

But dreams of heaven in the sky began to lose their universal appeal as the Age of Faith declined, and new dreams began to take shape—dreams of heaven *on earth* this time, dreams of revolution, dreams of turning everything upside down, of casting down the rulers of the past and raising up new rulers out of the ruled.

Many such revolutions occurred, most notably in France, America, and Russia, but in every case, strangely enough, the hierarchy merely changed hands and went on as before. The masses still have their stones to drag, day after day, and day after day the pyramids keep going up.

French philosopher Simone Weil disagreed with Marx, saying that revolution, not religion, is the opium of the masses. Shame on them both for not understanding people and their drugs better. Religion is a barbiturate, dulling the pain and putting you to sleep. Revolution is an amphetamine, revving you up and making you feel powerful. When people have nothing else going for them, they'll grab either one—or both. Neither drug is going away. Far from it. Contrary to postwar expectations, which saw religion slipping into the past like snake-oil medicine shows, religion is on the rise, right along with revolution. And in what is supposedly the happiest, most prosperous nation in human history, more and more antigovernment terrorist groups attract more and more members every year.

Opium is the opium of the people

When Marx made his famous pronouncement, opium itself was not a drug of the people, so what he was getting at is that religion is the public's cheap narcotic. He could not have guessed, perhaps, that opium itself (in one form or another) would eventually become the opium of the people, despite its cost.

As things get worse and worse for us, we're going to need more and more of all the things that give us relief and oblivion and all the things that get us revved up and excited. More religion, more revolution, more drugs, more television channels, more sports, more casinos, more pornography, more lotteries, more access to the Web—more and more and more of it all—to give ourselves the impression that life is nonstop fun. But meanwhile, of course, every morning we must shake off the hangover and forget about fun for eight or ten hours while we drag our quota of stones up the side of the pyramid.

What life could possibly be sweeter than this?

My own life at the pyramid

Readers are bound to be curious about my own working life. Have I, they must wonder, suffered so much as a stone-dragger? No, in fact, I've been one of the lucky ones. Early on I found a niche wherein I could think of myself as an artisan rather than a mere draft animal. You might say I dressed stones for others to drag, and I was proud of my workmanship. I began my working life on a nice, respectable little pyramid being built by Spencer Publishing in Chicago, called *The American Peoples Encyclopedia;* this was bought by a much larger builder, Grolier, which moved it stone by stone to New York City. I stayed behind in Chicago to work for Science Research Associates on a pyramid called the Greater Cleveland Mathematics Program. SRA too was soon bought by a bigger builder, IBM. I eventually moved on to the Encyclopaedia Britannica Educational Corporation, where I supervised pyramid building in the mathematics department. I ended my career at a company owned by another giant, the Singer Corporation, where I supervised all multimedia pyramid-building. The end there came when one day the president of the company told me my work was "too good." It didn't have to be that good, he explained, because it was "just for kids," and kids "don't know the difference." I finally realized I'd never be able to accomplish my goals working on anybody else's pyramids.

Am I building my own pyramid?

The craft I ply today is the one I plied for the companies I just mentioned. I'm not doing anything different for myself than I did for them. The work is the same . . . but I don't think it has anything to do with building a pyramid.

The test is this. If you had a billion dollars in the bank, would you go on doing the work you do to make a living? Really, honestly, truly? I'm sure about ten percent of the people reading this book would say yes—for example, Steven Spielberg and Bill Gates (who already has his billion but still seems to love his work). I too am among that lucky ten percent. If I had a billion in the bank, I'd go right on writing.

There's plenty of room in the world for the ten percent who love their work. My passion is to make a little room in the world for the other ninety percent who don't. I'm not trying to take away the fun that the Spielbergs and Gateses have, I'm trying to open an escape route for the billions who are *not* having fun, who slog stones up the pyramids not because they love stones or pyramids but because they have no other way to put food on the table. We can give them a break without taking away the break enjoyed by the lucky ten percent—but only if we go beyond this thing called civilization.

What does "civilization" mean?

I can name a couple of concepts I personally find slippery (*mise en scène*, for example, and *postmodernism*), but *civilization* isn't one of them. The *Oxford English Dictionary* handles it in a mere dozen words: "Civilized condition or state; a developed or advanced state of human society." The *American Heritage Dictionary* articulates it a bit more fully: "An advanced state of intellectual, cultural, and material development in human society, marked by progress in the arts and sciences, the extensive use of writing, and the appearance of complex political and social institutions."

The thing that forces the institutions of any civilization to become politically and socially "complex" is of course their hierarchical arrangement. A confederation of farming villages isn't politically and socially complex, and it's not a civilization. When, a thousand years later, the royal family lives in a palace guarded by professional soldiers and buffered from the masses by clans of nobles and a priestly caste that manages the state religion, then you have the requisite political and social "complexity"—and you have civilization.

No tribal society, no matter how "advanced" in other respects, has ever been called a civilization in this sense.

Putting the pieces together

The tribal life and no other is the gift of natural selection to humanity. It is to humanity what pack life is to wolves, pod life is to whales, and hive life is to bees. After three or four million years of human evolution, it alone emerged as the social organization that works for people. People like the tribal organization because it works equally well for all members.

Wherever civilization emerges, tribalism withers and is replaced by hierarchalism. Hierarchalism works very well for the rulers but much less well for the ruled, who make up the mass of the society. For this reason, the few at the top like it very well and the masses at the bottom like it very much less well.

With one exception, the experience of history is that people who make a trial of the hierarchal life ultimately abandon it as unsatisfactory. Some trials were still in progress when we destroyed them, so we can't know how they might have ended otherwise. We're the one exception. We're driven to cling to our hierarchical society by a complex of memes that tell us that what we have is unimprovable no matter how much we dislike it, no matter if it devastates the world and results in our own extinction. These memes tell us that what we have is the life humans were meant to have from the beginning and cannot be bettered by any other.

Another experiment in hierarchalism

The Natchez, a people found by seventeenth-century Europeans to be flourishing in the area around modern Natchez, Mississippi, had a society rather midway between a federation of farming villages and a full-blown theocratic civilization like that of the Egyptians or Maya. They had three classes of nobles and one class of commoners. At the top were the Suns, the chief of whom was a living god, the Great Sun. Next came the Nobles, then the Honored People. The commoners at the bottom were the Stinkards.

What makes the Natchez experiment noteworthy is the fact that the classes were hereditary, but membership in them wasn't (or at least not exactly), because every member of the nobility was required to marry a Stinkard. This meant that every member of the Stinkard class saw its children rise a notch, while every member of the nobility saw its children sink a notch. Passing over the details, the effect of marrying into the Stinkard class was this, that the son of a Sun was a Noble (not a Sun), and the son of this Noble was an Honored (not a Noble), while the son of this Honored was a Stinkard. But having reached the bottom of the social scale, this great-grandson of a Sun was now eligible to marry a Sun woman, and their offspring would be a Sun, thus beginning the cycle all over again.

A systemic problem

In the Natchez system, no matter how exalted you were, one of your parents was a Stinkard—and even if you were at the bottom of the heap, you could marry a noble and have noble children. It's hard to imagine how such a bizarre system could have evolved in the ordinary way. I presume it was a deliberate contrivance, intended to correct the perceived flaw that caused hierarchical systems elsewhere to be abandoned. Perhaps the Natchez consciously perceived it as a way to fix what was wrong with societies like the Mayan and the Olmec. If so, the Natchez may have made the greatest discovery in the history of human social development—a way to build a hierarchical society that was actually tolerable to all its members, because no family ever found itself stuck at the bottom but was constantly revolving through the hierarchy. Would natural selection have rewarded the system with survival? Would the Natchez have held onto their members? Sadly, we'll never know, because they were wiped out by the French at the end of the seventeenth century.

As promising as this system seems, however, it had a fundamental flaw. Because all three noble classes had to marry into the lowest class, marriageable Stinkards were chronically in short supply and had to be augmented with captives from conquered neighbors. With this systemic impetus toward conquest, the Natchez might (with a few thousand years head start) have become the conquerors of the world instead of us—and might now be facing exactly our sort of crisis.

Beyond hierarchalism

Every civilization brought forth in the course of human history has been a hierarchical affair. The thing we call civilization goes hand in hand with hierarchy—*means* hierarchy, *requires* hierarchy. Why this is so would make a fascinating study—but, again, not my study. It's enough for me to know that it *is* so. You can have hierarchy without civilization, but you can't have civilization without hierarchy; at least we never have—not once, not anywhere, in ten thousand years of civilization building. To have a civilization is to have a hierarchical society.

To go beyond civilization therefore means going beyond hierarchalism.

Does going beyond civilization mean destroying civilization? Certainly not. Why would it?

All dedicated pyramid-builders should stick with civilization. The rest of us just want something else, and it's high time we had it.

A wrong direction: "giving up" things

Despite all the indicators of misery we live with—the ever-growing incidence of social disintegration, drug addiction, crime, suicide, mental illness, child and spousal abuse and abandonment, racism, violence against women, and so on—most people in our culture are thoroughly convinced that our way of life simply cannot be bettered by any means whatever. Adopting anything different would therefore have to be a come-down, an act of sacrifice.

Very typically, when people question me about the future, they ask if I really believe people will be willing to "give up" the wonderful things we have for the mere privilege of avoiding extinction. When I speak, as I did in *Ishmael,* of "another story to be in," they seem to imagine I'm touting a sort of miserable half-life of voluntary poverty, donning sackcloth and ashes to do penance for our environmental sins. They're sure that living in a sustainable way must be about "giving up" things. It doesn't occur to them that living in an UNsustainable way is *also* about giving up things, very precious things like security, hope, light-heartedness, and freedom from anxiety, fear, and guilt.

When in doubt, think about the circus. People never run off to join the circus to *give up* something. They run off to the cir-cus to *get* something.

Standards of living

Anthropologist Marshall Sahlins has written: "The world's most primitive people have few possessions, *but they are not poor.* Poverty is not a certain small amount of goods, nor is it just a relation between means and ends; above all it is a relation between people. Poverty is a social status. As such it is the invention of civilization."

My wife, Rennie, and I learned this great truth for ourselves during the 1980s, in the seven years we spent in Madrid, a mountain village in central New Mexico. Eking out a living on a small inheritance, I was at work on the book that would some-day become *Ishmael.* During this time we were poor by ordinary standards but just ordinary by Madrid standards. In Madrid at this time *everyone* was poor—and so *no one* was poor. The average Madrid *household* income was probably around three thousand dollars—vastly below the national poverty level—but there were no poor people in Madrid. No one gloried in being poor or in living "simply." All gloried in their independence, in their ingenuity, in their acquisition of needed skills, and above all in doing what they *wanted* to do.

Visitors to Madrid (doubtless like visitors to circus back lots) probably had the impression that it was a sort of "depressed area." In fact, I've never lived in an area that was less depressed!

Standards of living: Chicago–Madrid

When Rennie and I moved from Chicago to Madrid, we recognized in a vague way that we were lowering our standard of living, but we weren't doing this to make ourselves harmless or to reduce our impact on the planet. We were doing it to reduce our expenses while I was working on the book that ultimately became *Ishmael.*

To give you an idea of the difference, in nearby Santa Fe at this time you quite literally couldn't buy a rundown one-car garage for $80,000. In nearby Madrid, by contrast, we were able to buy a nice little building right on the highway that was serving as both living quarters and a general store, complete with inventory, for $30,000. Even at this price I'm not sure we would have bought it if it hadn't been situated in a way that suited us perfectly. The principal element of that situation was that it was on the town's main street and within easy walking distance of all the town's urban resources (modest as they were). In these respects, it was just like our previous residence, in Chicago, where we lived on Lake Shore Drive, within easy walking distance of all the resources of the Belmont Harbor/New Town area. By leaving Chicago and moving to Madrid, we managed to get *more* of what we needed at that time by *lowering* our standard of living.

Standards of living: Madrid–Houston

Another element of the Madrid house that suited us was the fact that it had a large room (which most people would think of as a living room) that served us as twin offices spaced far enough apart that we were not working in each other's lap but close enough so we could communicate easily.

Today, some twelve years later, we live on a main thoroughfare, within easy walking distance of the urban resources of a major city. One of the things that suits us about our residence is that it has a large room (which most people would think of as a living room) that serves us as twin offices spaced far enough apart that we're not working in each other's lap but close enough so we can communicate easily.

Needless to say, there are some things available to us in Houston that were not available in Madrid, and these are things we need in our present circumstances, which are very different now. Roughly speaking, by moving to Houston we've upped our standard of living by a factor of ten over the Madrid years. What has *not* been upped is our overall feeling of contentment and well-being. If we're happier today (and we are), it has nothing to do with our higher standard of living.

Spending more will certainly get you more, but it won't necessarily get you more of what you *want*.

A lover of civilization

People who dislike what I'm saying will often try to reassure themselves with the thought that I'm just someone who hates civilization and would rather live "close to nature." This will bring a smile to the face of anyone who knows me, for I'm a great lover of civilization and live happily in the heart of the fourth largest U.S. city, in easy walking distance to drugstores, supermarkets, video rental shops, art galleries, restaurants, bookstores, museums, pool halls, universities, and tattoo parlors. (And I live "close to nature" every second of every day, 365 days a year, since "nature" is something no one can escape living close to, no matter where you happen to live.)

Or they challenge me to say how I'd like living without air conditioning, central heating, indoor plumbing, refrigerators, telephones, computers, and so on. They think I'm an apostle of poverty, though they can't point to a single word in any of my writings to support such a notion.

I'm not a Luddite or a Unabomber. I don't regard civilization as a curse but as a blessing that people (including me) should be free to walk away from—for something better. And something better is what I'm after, and nothing less. Those who are looking for something *worse* definitely need to consult a different book.

Searching for an alternative

Consulting any dictionary reveals that the word *civilization* signifies to us something that is socially "advanced." There is, of course, only one thing for it to be socially advanced *over*, and that's tribalism. (Barbarianism doesn't represent a specific type of social organization; barbarians are either tribal people or people at a stage of civilization perceived to be more primitive than one's own.)

In our cultural mythology we see ourselves as having left tribalism behind the way modern medicine left the leech and the bleeding bowl behind, and we did so decisively and irrevocably. This is why it's so difficult for us to acknowledge that tribalism is not only the preeminently *human* social organization, it's also the only unequivocally *successful* social organization in human history. Thus, when even so wise and thoughtful a statesman as Mikhail Gorbachev calls for "a new beginning" and "a new civilization," he doesn't doubt for a single moment that the pattern for it lies in the social organization that has introduced humanity to oppression, injustice, poverty, chronic famine, incessant violence, genocide, global warfare, crime, corruption, and wholesale environmental destruction. To consult, in our time of deepest crisis, with the unqualified success that humanity enjoyed here for more than three million years is quite simply and utterly unthinkable.

That, finally, is my purpose in this book: to think about the utterly unthinkable.

PART FOUR

Toward the New Tribalism

We are inclined to think of hunters and gatherers as *poor* because they don't have anything; perhaps better to think of them for that reason as *free*.

MARSHALL SAHLINS

Revolution without upheaval

Because revolution in our culture has always represented an attack on hierarchy, it has always meant upheaval—literally a heaving up from below. But upheaval has no role to play in moving beyond civilization. If the plane is in trouble, you don't shoot the pilot, you grab a parachute and jump. To overthrow the hierarchy is pointless; we just want to leave it behind.

As everyone knows (especially revolutionaries), hierarchy maintains formidable defenses against attack from the lower orders. It has none, however, against abandonment. This is in part because it can imagine revolution, but it can't imagine abandonment. But even if it could imagine abandonment, it couldn't defend against it, because abandonment isn't an attack, it's just a discontinuance of support.

It's almost impossible to prevent people from doing nothing (which is what discontinuing support amounts to).

But won't the powers that be *try* to prevent people from doing nothing? I can imagine them *trying* (but I honestly need help imagining them *succeeding*).

Revolution without overthrow

The object of ordinary revolution is to effect global change across the board with a single, sweeping blow. Ideally, former rulers must disappear overnight—en masse, along with all supporters and minions—with a complete cast of successors ready to step into their shoes the following morning to proclaim the new regime. Scenarios like this one are meaningless to those who would move beyond civilization.

In the first place, there's no need for global change. Those who insist on having nothing less than global change will wait a long time, probably forever. There's no need for everyone in the world to go to bed one night living one way and wake up the next morning living another way. This isn't going to happen, and it's pointless to try to make it happen.

There is likewise no need for change across the board—for everything to suddenly begin to be done differently. It's unnecessary for this to happen, and nothing in the world can make it happen. Always keep in mind that *there is no one right way for people to live.* There never has been and never will be.

Finally, we don't want the ruling class to disappear overnight. We're not ready to see the infrastructure of civilization disappear (and may never be). At least for the time being, we want our rulers and leaders to continue to supervise civilization's drudgery for us—keeping the potholes filled, the sewage and water treatment plants running, and so on.

DANIEL QUINN

No one right way

People often imagine that it would be wonderful if all six billion of us started living a new way tomorrow. It's one of our most deep-rooted and misguided memes, that there absolutely must be some one right way for *everyone* to live.

I admire the Gebusi of New Guinea, but (trust me) not everyone in the world should live the way they do. I admire the Gypsies, but not everyone in the world should live the way they do—and (oddly enough) if they did, their way of life would fail. I admire the Jalali—nomadic peddlers and performers of Afghanistan—but not everyone in the world should live the way they do. I admire the Tuposa of the Sudan, the Rendille of Kenya, and the Kariera of Western Australia, but not everyone in the world should live the way they do. This isn't sociological thinking, this is ecological thinking. Macaws have a good life, but their habitats would fail if all birds lived like macaws. Giraffes have a good life, but their habitats would fail if all mammals lived like giraffes. Beavers have a good life, but their habitats would fail if all rodents lived like beavers.

Diversity, not uniformity, is what works. Our problem is not that people are living a *bad* way but rather that they're all living the *same* way. The earth can accommodate many people living in a voraciously wasteful and pollutive way, it just can't accommodate *all* of us living that way.

No heavenly choir

We don't need to have all six billion of us living like environmental saints tomorrow—or ever, for that matter. To take such a thing as our objective would merely assure failure. This is precisely the strength of the strategy I'm proposing here. We don't need to achieve the impossible dreams of global enlightenment, unity, and resolve that people like Mikhail Gorbachev and Al Gore describe as humanity's only hope. We simply can't, as Gorbachev suggests, wait for "all members of the world community" to "resolutely discard old stereotypes." We can't wait for all members of the world community to do *anything*, because if we know anything at all, we know that all members of the world community will never, ever do *anything* as a body. "The time has come," Gorbachev says, "to choose a new direction of global development." But who's going to do this choosing? Everyone? And how many decades (or even centuries) will have to pass before that happens? Where on earth is Al Gore's "New Common Purpose" to come from? When have the people of earth ever been able to agree on a common *anything?* These are will-o'-the-wisps, vain expectations that keep us rooted in hopelessness, year after year, decade after decade.

We can't wait for our national leaders to save us. When all we demand from them (or even tolerate from them) are instant, short-term gains, why would they suddenly begin thinking like global visionaries?

Those who would wait

Because we don't expect to overthrow governments, abolish world capitalism, make civilization vanish, or turn everyone in the world into walking buddhas, we don't have to wait for *anything*. But I have to warn you that many people will tell you the opposite, that we have to wait until we have a world that is *already* perfect. They feel absolutely nothing should happen until we've banished social inequality, racism, sexism, poverty, and every other bad thing you can think of.

I've had people tell me we have to wait till everyone "respects" everyone else. I've had people tell me we can't do anything till everyone's "consciousness" has been raised. People who think like this would wait for the cut to heal before applying a bandage, would wait till daybreak to light a candle, would wait for the sinking ship to rise before getting in the lifeboat. They're way past my comprehension, and beyond offering the opinion that they're going to have an awful long wait, I can't think of a thing to say to them.

Fighters of the good fight

A friend recently sent me a copy of *Deep Democracy*, a periodical published by the Alliance for Democracy, whose mission is "to free all people from corporate domination of politics, economics, the environment, culture, and information; to establish true democracy; and to create a just society with a sustainable equitable economy." The cover featured an illustration in political-cartoon style of the organization's self-perception: a diminutive David facing a Goliath armed with the sword of money politics and the spear of greed, wearing the armor of multinational corporations, and shielded by a mainstream media monopoly. The title of the cartoon couldn't have been more apt: "Déjà Vu (All Over Again)." Indeed. Over and over and over and over.

I had to explain to my friend that, while I wish the Alliance the best of luck, I don't perceive myself to be a participant in this struggle. We can't afford to wait for David to finish off Goliath, because obviously David *never* finishes off Goliath. The two of them have been standing there toe to toe for thousands of years—and they'll still be standing there a thousand years from now.

We don't need to defeat Goliath. We need to change the way he thinks.

Goliath with a new mind

Once upon a time in the commercial carpeting industry there was a Goliath named Ray C. Anderson who had taken his company, Interface, Inc., from a modest beginning to a position of global leadership in about twenty years, becoming one of those wicked billionaire multinational corporations you hear about. This Goliath had always made a point of being in compliance with government regulations, but these didn't stop the business from being a highly pollutive one—petroleum based and contributing heavily to landfill.

But in 1994 he read two books that *changed his mind* about what he was doing. One was Paul Hawken's book, *The Ecology of Commerce,* the other was *Ishmael.* After reading these books, Ray Anderson saw that *being in compliance* is not nearly enough. He immediately initiated action to end his dependence on petroleum and to begin making one hundred percent recyclable carpeting made from one hundred percent recycled materials, thus reducing his company's contribution to landfill to zero. It's important to note that these changes didn't affect just his corporation. Suddenly all his competitors were compelled to adopt *his* standards in order to remain competitive. This Goliath didn't just reform a business, he reformed an entire industry—not because any plucky little David defeated him, but because two books made him think a different way about the world and his place in it.

If people will *willingly* reform an industry when their minds are changed, why spend billions to enact and enforce laws to *compel* them to do it?

The incremental revolution

I say again that, because we don't expect to overthrow governments, abolish world capitalism, make civilization vanish, turn everyone in the world into walking buddhas, or cure all social and economic ills, we don't have to wait for *anything*. If ten people walk beyond civilization and build a new sort of life for themselves, then those ten are *already* living in the next paradigm, from the first day. They don't need the support of an organization. They don't need to belong to a party or a movement. They don't need new laws to be passed. They don't need permits. They don't need a constitution. They don't need tax-exempt status.

For those ten, the revolution will already have succeeded.

They probably should be prepared, however, for the outrage of their neighbors.

Ethnic tribalism won't work for us

The tribes we grew up with during the first three or four million years of human life were ethnic groups, extended families having a common language, common laws and customs, and so on. Their social borders were generally (but not absolutely) closed to members of other tribes. Captives of war were an obvious exception, but a member of the Sioux, for example, couldn't ordinarily just decide to become a Navajo. It might happen under extraordinary circumstances, to be sure, but tribal integrity would have suffered if it became a general rule.

Rennie and I have links to the Quinn clan and to the MacKay clan (hers), but like most modern clan members, we go our way and they go theirs. Very occasionally what might be considered a tribal action will take place in these clans, but in the modern world no one is surprised when people turn out to be closer to friends and colleagues than to families.

But there's nothing specially sacrosanct about ethnic tribalism. The sort of tribalism we see at work in the circus evolved in the same way as ethnic tribalism. It too is the product of natural selection, works as well (in its own way) as ethnic tribalism, and provides us with a model that is perfectly adapted to the urban circumstances most of us find ourselves in.

Jeffrey

In *My Ishmael* I recounted the life of a young man named Jeffrey, loosely based on Paul Eppinger, whose journal was published by his father under the title *Restless Mind Quiet Thoughts*. Jeffrey was attractive, intelligent, personable, and multitalented, but he couldn't find anything he wanted to do, other than hang out with friends, write in his journal, and play the guitar. His friends were forever urging him to find a direction, get some ambition, and *care* about something, but of course none of these things can be done at will. He came to believe his friends when they told him he was unusual—peculiar, even—in his aimlessness. In the end, despairing of finding the purposefulness that seems to come so easily to others, he quietly and without fuss took his own life.

I wasn't surprised to hear from many youngsters who feel exactly like Jeffrey, who know the world is full of things they *should* want to do—and who imagine that there must be something dreadfully wrong with them for failing to want it. Because I've taken the trouble to study cultures different from our own, I know there's nothing innately human about wanting to "make something" of yourself or to "get ahead" or to have a career, a profession, or a vocation. Notions like these are foreign to most aboriginal peoples, who seem perfectly content to live just the way Jeffrey wanted to live—and why shouldn't they be?

The open tribe

Jeffrey died for lack of a tribe—but not, of course, for lack of an ethnic tribe. Youngsters often tell me they long to run off to join the Yanomami of Brazil or the Alawa of Australia, and I have to explain that tribes like these aren't open to them. Though famously hospitable, they can't afford to take in wide-eyed kids who show up on their doorsteps completely devoid of the skills needed to help the tribe survive.

Throughout his wanderings, Jeffrey stayed with people who were making a living of one kind or another—family friends, ex-college chums, their parents, and so on. But, not surprisingly, none of them were making a living *tribally;* they had jobs, professions, and careers, but these were held *individually,* so there was no room for Jeffrey in them. They weren't making a living as a collaborative effort, so there was no way to extend their living to him. He was forever a guest, and guests (however charming) inevitably wear out their welcome.

In a sense, Jeffrey was unable to find anyone who knew how to give him as *little* as he wanted. Many youngsters want as little, and if they'll work together tribally, they can get it quite easily. Every tribe has the standard of living its members are *willing* to support.

People like Jeffrey need to live in a world of tribes, and a world of *open* tribes. And they aren't alone in this. Far from it, I think.

The limits of openness

The circus is the very model of an open tribe. Things like nationality, language, race, ethnic background, age, gender, sexual orientation, political opinions, and religious beliefs won't exclude anyone who can contribute to the living of the circus, but its openness isn't absolute, of course. It isn't a refuge for the homeless, for example; it doesn't take in people altruistically. This isn't to say that there's a prohibition against altruism. The circus must take good care of its members or they'll defect to circuses that are more open-handed and bountiful. It's a question of survival. A species that can't hold onto its members becomes extinct, and the same is true of a tribe.

On the other hand, a circus that is too altruistic (for example, that takes in people who don't contribute to its success) soon has difficulty making ends meet; it begins cutting salaries, lowering the general living standard, skimping on quality across the board—and begins to lose its most talented members to other circuses.

Circuses that find a workable balance between economic success and community needs stay in business. Circuses that don't find that balance disappear.

Nontribal businesses

Ordinary businesses don't burden themselves with tribal obligations. Most obviously, they don't "take care" of their workers; to do so would introduce them to a whole suite of problems in which there's no profit whatever. Instead, they pay salaries and expect workers to take care of themselves. One worker may thrive on a given salary, while another languishes on it. From the company's point of view, there's no injustice in this if the salary is fair in the first place. It's not the company's fault that the second worker has a large family to support or an ailing parent to take care of—or is just a bad manager of money. The company can afford to be hard-nosed about this; it doesn't risk losing this second worker to a competitor, because its competitors are equally hard-nosed about it.

This unspoken agreement among businesses to limit their obligation to issuing a paycheck is precisely what gives our society its prison ambience. Workers have "no way out." Whether they move from company to company or from nation to nation, their employers' obligation ends with the paycheck (an arrangement that obviously suits employers very well). Prisons are always arranged to suit the warders. That's the anticipated order of things. No one thinks that prisons are built to suit the needs of prisoners or that businesses are built to suit the needs of workers.

Stepping into a tribe means stepping out of the prison.

But how does it render us harmless?

Having read this far, a student said to me, "I love what you're saying, but I don't see how just walking away from civilization helps us live 'as harmlessly as sharks and tarantulas and rattlesnakes,' which is the benchmark for success you established in *Ishmael*."

I think that, like many people, this person is more at ease with the idea of giving up things than getting things. He worries that people enjoying themselves may not be living as blamelessly as people denying themselves. Well-intentioned people often want to feel they're giving up something, which is only to be expected in a culture where all ethical and religious systems commend self-denial. In hierarchical societies it's always a good idea to make poverty sound like a blessing (and the rich are always especially vain about their austerities).

If you think this is something that no longer holds true, try this. Find me a single elementary or secondary textbook that promotes *being rich* as a value. Being rich is *never* held up to schoolchildren as an ideal. Look all you want, you won't find a single text that says: "Make lots of money so you can have the best of everything—exotic cars, luxurious mansions, yachts, servants, designer clothes, extravagant jewelry, endless first-class travel, and so on." Our official classroom mythology is as prissy about wealth as it is about sex.

"The culture of maximum harm"

People have lived many different ways on this planet, but about ten thousand years ago there appeared one people who believed everyone in the world should live a single way—*their* way, which they considered the only "right" way. After ten thousand years of hard work, this one people, whom I've called the Takers, had conquered every continent on the planet and dominated the world completely. In the course of their conquest, the Takers overran, swallowed up, displaced, or eliminated every other culture and civilization in their path. Once the civilizations of the New World were destroyed, there was only one civilization left in the entire world—that of the Takers: ours. From that point on, *civilization* was synonymous with *our civilization*.

At the present time, the United States represents the high point of maximum affluence that our civilization has reached. There's no place on earth where people have more, use more, or waste more than the United States. Though other nations haven't as yet reached this high point, they yearn to reach it. They have no other goal. There's only one right way for people to live, and the people of the United States epitomize it. Everyone in the world should have a house, a car, a computer, a television set, a telephone, and so on—at least one of each, preferably several.

This I call "the culture of maximum harm," a culture in which all members are dedicated to attaining the high point of maximum affluence (and to forever *raising* the high point of maximum affluence).

But how can we contain their expansion?

I've been asked, "If we don't crush the Taker way entirely, won't it rebound and begin expanding again?"

The Middle Ages could only remain the Age of Faith for as long as Christian mythology dominated people's minds, all the way from serfs to kings. After that mythology was abased and superceded during the Renaissance, it was inconceivable that such an Age of Faith could recur. Never again will a whole civilization embrace the vision that dominated the Middle Ages.

The same is true of Taker mythology. Once it has been exposed for what it is—a collection of poisonous delusions—it will no longer be capable of exercising the power it has exercised over us for the past ten thousand years. Who, knowing that there's no one right way for people to live, will take up the sword to spread the Taker vision? Who, knowing that civilization is *not* humanity's last invention, will defend the hierarchy as if it were humanity's most sacred institution?

But won't the last pharaohs in their maddened wrath turn their nuclear arsenal on us?

Perhaps they would if they could, but where are they going to find us except living right beside them in their own cities? Is the president, seeing his/her power slip away, going to bomb Washington D.C. to destroy the tribal people living there? Is the governor of New York going to bomb Manhattan?

Something better to hope for

Because all six billion members of the culture of maximum harm are striving to maximize their affluence, we shouldn't be alarmed solely by the one percent who live like lords of the universe. We must be equally alarmed by the other ninety-nine percent who are *hoping* to live like lords of the universe. It's probably not going to be the billionaire pop stars, sports heroes, and deal-makers who are going to lead us out of the prison we share with them. It's the rest of us who must find the way out, who must discover something better to hope for than inhabiting a sable-lined cell next to Barbra Streisand, Michael Jordan, or Donald Trump.

The world can support a few million pharaohs, but it can't support six billion pharaohs.

"Something better to hope for . . ." Is this by any chance a reference to what I called "another story to be in" in *Ishmael?* Is this what I meant when I said that "people need a vision of the world and of themselves that inspires them"? Is this what I meant when I said in *The Story of B* that "If the world is saved, it will be saved because the people living in it have a new vision"?

Of course it is.

An intermediate goal: less harmful

In case it isn't evident, I'm still working on my student's question: "How does walking away from civilization help us live as harmlessly as sharks and tarantulas and rattlesnakes?" Any move beyond civilization represents a move away from the culture of maximum harm and therefore reduces your harmfulness. Jumping over the wall of the prison won't instantly make you as harmless as a shark, tarantula, or rattlesnake, but it will instantly move you in that direction.

Look at it this way: no move beyond civilization will ever result in *greater* harm. If you want to do harm, you've *got* to stick to civilization. It's only inside that framework that you can burn up ten thousand gallons of jet fuel just to have lunch at your favorite restaurant in Paris. It's only inside that framework that you can casually dynamite a coral reef just because it inconveniences you.

Moving beyond civilization automatically limits your access to the tools needed to do harm. The people of the Circus Flora will never build a Stealth bomber or open a steel mill—not just because they wouldn't want to but because even if they wanted to, they wouldn't have access to the tools. To regain access to the tools, they'd have to leave the circus and find new places for themselves in the culture of maximum harm.

But is "less harmful" enough?

Though it's a good and necessary start, being less harmful is *not* enough. We're in the midst of a food race that is more deadly to us and to the world around us than the Cold War arms race was. This is a race between food production and population growth. Present-day followers of English economist Thomas Malthus (1766–1834), like those of the past, view producing enough food to feed our population as a "win," just as American Cold Warriors saw producing enough weapons to destroy the Soviet Union as a "win." They fail to see that, just as every American "win" stimulated an answering Soviet "win," every win in food production stimulates an answering "win" in population growth.

Right now our food race is rapidly converting our planet's biomass into *human* mass. This is what happens when we clear a piece of land of wildlife and replant it with human crops. This land was supporting a biomass comprising hundreds of thousands of species and tens of millions of individuals. Now all the productivity of that land is being turned into human mass, literally into human flesh. Every day all over the world diversity is disappearing as more and more of our planet's biomass is being turned into human mass. This is what the food race is about. This is *exactly* what the food race is about: every year turning more of our planet's biomass into human mass.

Ending the food race

The arms race could only be ended in two ways, either by a nuclear catastrophe or by the participants walking away from it. Luckily, the second of these happened. The Soviets called it quits—and there was no catastrophe.

The race between food and population is the same. It can be ended by catastrophe, when simply too much of our planet's biomass is tied up in humans, and fundamental ecological systems collapse, but it doesn't *have* to end that way. It can end the way the arms race ended, by people simply walking away from it. We can say, "We understand now that there can be *no final triumph* of food over population. This is because every single win made on the side of food is answered by a win on the side of population. It has to be that way, it always *has* been that way, and we can see that it's never going to *stop* being that way."

But this isn't going to happen because of these few words—or even the thousands I've devoted to it in my other books and speeches. This subject engages our cultural mythology at the most profound level—a level far deeper than I imagined when I thought it could be handled in a few pages in *Ishmael*. This is the deadly man-eating Minotaur at the center of the labyrinth of our culture . . . far beyond the scope of the present expedition.

100 years beyond civilization

People will still be living here in one hundred years—*if* we start living a new way, soon.

Otherwise, not.

But how would we get there, and what would it look like? Utopians can't let go of the idea of sweeter, gentler, more loving people taking over. I prefer to look at what worked for millions of years for people *as they are.* Sainthood was not required.

To project into the future: as people begin going over the wall in the early decades of the new millennium, our societal guardians are at first alarmed, seeing it as portending the end of civilization-as-we-know-it. They try heightening the wall with social and economic barbed wire but soon realize the futility of this. People will keep dragging stones if they're convinced there's no other way to go, but once another way opens up, nothing can stop them from defecting. Initially the defectors derive their living from the pyramid-builders, just as circuses do today. As time goes on, however, they begin to be less dependent on the pyramid-builders. They interact more and more with each other, building their own intertribal economy.

After a hundred years civilization is still hanging on at about half its present size. Half the world's population still belongs to the culture of maximum harm, but the other half, living tribally, enjoys a more modest lifestyle, directed toward getting more of what people want (as opposed to just getting more).

200 years beyond civilization

Gradually the economic balance of power shifts between "civilization" (by now almost always burdened with those quote marks) and the surrounding "beyond civilization." More and more people are seeing that they can trade off a plenitude of things they don't deeply want (power, social status, and supposed conveniences, amenities, and luxuries) for things they really do deeply want (security, meaningful work, more leisure, and social equality—all products of the tribal way of life). "The economy," no longer tied to an ever-expanding market, has become an increasingly local affair as global and national corporations gradually lose their reason for being.

Two hundred years out, the thing we call civilization has been left behind and seems as quaintly obsolete as Oliver Cromwell's theocracy. The cities are still there—where would they go?—as are the arts, the sciences, and technology, but these are no longer instruments and embodiments of the culture of maximum harm.

I don't indulge in these speculations in order to lay claim to powers of prophecy. I toss them into the water to show you what part of the pond I'm aiming at . . . and to let you follow the ripples back to the shore of the present.

But where exactly is "beyond"?

In the paradigmatic utopian scenario, you gather your friends, equip yourselves with agricultural tools, and find a bit of wilderness paradise to which you can escape and get away from it all. The apparent attraction of this weary old fantasy is that it requires no imagination (being ready-made), can be enacted by almost anyone with the requisite funds, and sometimes actually works for longer than a few months. To advocate it as a general solution for six billion people would set an all-time record for inanity.

Civilization isn't a geographical territory, it's a social and economic territory where pharaohs reign and pyramids are built by the masses. Similarly, beyond civilization isn't a geographical territory, it's a social and economic territory where people in open tribes pursue goals that may or may not be recognizably "civilized."

You don't have to "go somewhere" to get beyond civilization. You have to make your living a different way.

PART FIVE ❋

The Tribe of Crow

Yeah,

Well,

It's pretty lonely

at the bottom,

too.

JOSEPH CHASSLER

Reluctant pioneers

By conservative estimates, at any one time there are about half a million people in the United States who have been thrust beyond civilization into a social and economic limbo that nowadays is identified as homelessness. Homelessness is slightly more than a euphemism for poverty, since it draws attention to the special form poverty takes in hypermodern cities, which might be defined as cities in which space is so valuable that none of it can be spared for the poor. With the complete disappearance of low-cost housing, there's just no room "indoors" for the poor in such cities.

Several distinct streams come together in the homeless flood. One consists of the mentally ill, turned out into the streets when deinstitutionalization became the rage in the 1970s. Another consists of semi- or unskilled workers whose jobs have been exported to countries where labor is cheaper or made superfluous by downsizing or automation. Another consists of those who in the fifties and sixties would have been called the "disadvantaged"—abandoned women and children, victims of racial or ethnic prejudice, undereducated, unskilled, and chronically unemployed. All these are perceived as victims or as the "deserving" poor. Others in the homeless flood are runaways, drug addicts, bums, winos, transients, and vagabonds, who, because they apparently "choose" to be homeless, are the "undeserving" poor.

Making the homeless disappear

Public officials (reflecting the unspoken desires of their constituents) naturally want the homeless to disappear. This isn't an unkind impulse. The assumption is that the homeless really *want* to disappear (at least the "deserving poor" among them)—by getting jobs, finding homes, and resuming a "normal" life. The role of officialdom is therefore to assist, prompt, and encourage the homeless to get about the business of resuming that normal life. Above all, nothing must be done that would encourage the homeless to *remain* homeless. In short, homelessness must be made as unremittingly difficult, degrading, and painful as possible, and you may be sure that our public guardians know well how to accomplish this.

Naturally the public wants homeless shelters, but these are hardly expected to be hospitable; no one should want to "stay" in one. If the homeless began to "stay" in shelters, this would defeat the purpose, which is to entice them out of homelessness. Avoiding officially sanctioned shelters at all costs, the homeless take refuge almost anywhere else—in alleys, parks, tunnels, and abandoned buildings, under bridges, and so on. The police have to roust them from these areas regularly, because if the homeless become comfortable *anywhere*, what motive have they to *stop* being homeless? Making and keeping the homeless as miserable as possible is cherished as a sort of tough love—the very best and kindest thing we can do for them.

The only trouble is, for some strange reason, it doesn't work worth a damn.

DANIEL QUINN

If it didn't work last year . . .

The greatest discovery any alien anthropologist could make about our culture is our overriding response to failure: *If it didn't work last year, do it AGAIN this year (and if possible do it MORE).*

Every year we pass more laws, hire more police, build more prisons, and sentence more offenders for longer periods—all without moving one inch closer to "ending" crime. It didn't work last year or the year before that or the year before that or the year before that, but you can be sure we'll try it again this year, knowing beyond a shadow of a doubt that it won't work this year either.

Every year we spend more money on our schools, hoping to "fix" whatever's wrong with them, and every year the schools remain stubbornly unfixed. Spending money didn't work last year or the year before that or the year before that or the year before that, but you can be sure we'll try it again this year, knowing beyond a shadow of a doubt that it won't work this year either.

Every year we try to make the homeless go away, and every year the homeless remain with us. We couldn't shoehorn them back into "the mainstream" last year or the year before that or the year before that or the year before that, but you can be sure we'll try it again this year, knowing beyond a shadow of a doubt that it won't work this year either.

A new rule for new minds

To figure out a better response to failure than this, you don't (as they say) have to be a rocket scientist. I'd formulate it this way: *If it didn't work last year or the year before that or the year before that—or any year in recorded history—then TRY SOMETHING DIFFERENT.*

We deeply believe in taking a military approach to problems. We proclaim a "war" on poverty. When that fails, we proclaim a "war" on drugs. We "fight" crime. We "combat" homelessness. We "battle" hunger. We vow to "defeat" AIDS.

Engineers can't afford to fail as consistently as politicians and bureaucrats, so they prefer accedence to resistance (as I do). For example, they know that no structure can be made rigid enough to resist an earthquake. So, rather than defy the earthquake's power by building rigid structures, they accede to it by building flexible ones. To accede is not merely to give in but rather to give in while drawing near; one may accede not only to an argument but to a throne. Thus the earthquake-proof building survives not by defeating the earthquake's power but by acknowledging it—by drawing it in and dealing with it.

As soon as someone is brave enough to deal with homelessness this way, by acknowledging it and drawing it in instead of fighting it, remarkable things will begin to happen in that place—and not just for the homeless.

Listening to the homeless

One element of acceding to homelessness is accepting the fact that the poor will consistently choose the least worst alternative available to them. If you find them living under a bridge instead of in a nice, clean municipal shelter just a block away, you can be absolutely sure they haven't made a mistake—from their point of view. The shelter's admittance procedures may be intolerably invasive, arbitrary, or humiliating, or its rules may be Draconian. Whatever, the discomforts of sheltering under the bridge are more endurable. Naturally what's least worst to one individual isn't necessarily the least worst to another. Street people in New York City will tell you there's so much food around it's almost impossible to starve. Even so, there are some who would rather shun that world of abundance and stay deep underground, where fresh game is plentiful (once you get used to the idea of hunting, killing, and cooking "track rabbits"—rats).

Another element of acceding to homelessness is accepting the fact that the homeless understand their situation, not necessarily the way a social scientist, economist, or urban planner would but from a practical and personal point of view. They may not be able to discourse on the process of deindustrialization, but they know that people who smugly order them to "get a job" are living in never-never land and imagining a world of work that hasn't existed in decades.

Is homelessness an earthquake?

A castaway in the sea was going down for the third time when he caught sight of a passing ship. Gathering his last strength, he waved frantically and called for help. Someone on board peered at him scornfully and shouted back, "Get a boat!"

Social Scientist Peter Marcuse has written: "Homelessness inspires not only the intellectual realization that the machinery of the system has failed somehow to produce basic shelter everyone needs, but even more the social realization that the system has come up against some limits it cannot exceed, has created *a world it can no longer control.*" (Emphasis added.)

I like this quote because its reference to "the machinery of the system" fits my engineering analogy so neatly. This machinery has created a world inhabited by people *it can no longer control.* To translate this into my own metaphorical system, Marcuse is saying the homeless have been pushed into a social and economic no man's land that is *beyond civilization.* And when that machinery exerts itself to force the homeless back where they belong, it fails—repeatedly and consistently.

Technology guru Jacques Attali has announced the end of the era of the working class. "Machines are the new proletariat," he says. "The working class is being given its walking papers." But we all know there's no room for nonworkers within the structure known as civilization. So where on earth are their walking papers supposed to take them—except *beyond* that structure?

What would acceding look like?

We know what "combating" homelessness looks like. We attack on two fronts. On one front, for example, we open shelters for the homeless but (since we don't want them to *stay* in the shelters) we make them as unwelcoming as possible. On the other front, we pass anticamping legislation that criminalizes those who *won't* stay in the shelters. This legislation allows (or compels) the police to harass the homeless, who are "out of place," who turn up where we don't want them to be. Until the homeless straighten out, get jobs, and somehow magically lift themselves into the mainstream of middle-class America, the game is going to be "Heads we win, tails you lose."

Acceding to homelessness would look like *helping the homeless succeed WHILE being homeless.* What an idea! I can almost hear the howls of outrage from both liberals and conservatives that must greet such a concept. Help people *succeed* at being homeless? We want them to *fail* at being homeless! (So they'll return to the mainstream.)

Step one in acceding to homelessness would be to decriminalize and deregulate the homeless. We can happily deregulate trillion-dollar industries capable of doing immense harm, but deregulating the relatively helpless poor—what a thought! The officers of deregulated savings and loan institutions may have bilked us out of billions, but at least they didn't hang around street corners in shabby clothes!

Letting them house themselves

Regulating and criminalizing homelessness is equivalent to defying earthquakes with rigid structures. Deregulating and decriminalizing homelessness is equivalent to acknowledging that "the machinery of the system has . . . created a world it can no longer control." We should abandon control of homelessness, therefore, because it's *beyond* control, just like the earthquake. Since we can't defeat it, we should learn to make the best of it.

There are thousands of miles of unused, habitable tunnels under Manhattan that are interdicted to the homeless for only one reason: that the homeless might try to live in them. The homeless *do* try to live in them, so it's conceived to be the duty of officialdom to drive them out. Officials explain that no one "should" live in the tunnels. They weren't designed as living spaces. They're unsafe. They're unhealthy. They're unsanitary. Despite all this, some of the homeless would *rather* live in the tunnels than in doorways or under bridges.

Instead of sending in the police to drive the homeless out of the tunnels, officials should send in city engineers to ask what services the city could provide to improve conditions. What they would hear is, "We need help with sanitation, with water, with electricity."

Don't try to drive the homeless into places *we* find suitable. Help them survive in places *they* find suitable.

Letting them feed themselves

Just as we want to deny the homeless access to shelter in tunnels, abandoned buildings, shack cities under bridges, and so on, we also want to deny them access to the plenitude of perfectly edible food that is discarded daily in our cities. Some restaurants have adopted the practice of dousing discarded food with ammonia to render it inedible. Others have installed locks on their dumpsters. Imagine instead helping the homeless organize systems to distribute this food, much of which now just ends up rotting in landfills.

Or, even better, imagine the outrage such a proposal would awaken in the good burghers of our cities. How dreadful (even immoral!) it would seem to them to allow a class of "loafers" to make a living out of what we no longer need or want. More than merely "allowing" such a way of life, we would actually be *encouraging* it—*facilitating* it!—when instead we should be "combating" it, stamping it out!

Letting them make a living

In our culture, for some odd reason, we teach kids to despise scavengers. Prey and predators are heroic, but scavengers are contemptible. The truth is, our world would be unlivable without scavengers. We'd be buried in corpses. Scavengers make their living by ridding the world of its biological refuse. Far from cursing them, we should bless them. Right now most road kills are made to disappear by birds like crows and vultures. If these birds ever become extinct, we ourselves will have to take over their duty. What these scavengers presently do for us at no cost, we'll have to pay for out of our pockets.

The only "honest" living available to the homeless in general is scavenging—and in general they're quite content to make that living. It's work they can do without having an address, submitting to supervision, punching a clock, or maintaining a wardrobe of socially approved clothing—and it's flex-time all the way.

David Wagner describes how teams of drunks work together to strip sellable copper from abandoned buildings in the northern city of his study. Naturally this is illegal, even though the copper would otherwise just be lost. Instead of obstructing this sort of activity as much as possible, why not facilitate it? Enormous amounts of materials could be reclaimed and recycled in this way, not only conserving resources but reducing the amount of material that goes into landfills to degenerate into toxic waste.

Let my people go!

The homeless are "beyond civilization" because they're beyond the reach of civilization's hierarchy, which has been unable to develop a structural extension to enclose them. The most it can manage is to oppress, harry, and obstruct them. To accede to homelessness would be to "let them go," much as the biblical pharaoh let the Israelites go.

Am I saying the homeless actually *want* to be homeless? Not exactly. Some are "short-termers" who have landed on the streets after a spell of bad luck and who want only to get back on the road to middle-class success. None of my proposals would hinder this. The rest are on the streets not necessarily because they love being homeless but because the alternatives are worse than being homeless—institutionalization, unending family abuse, involvement in foster-care systems that are blind or indifferent to their needs, and laboring in a job market that offers no real hope of upward mobility.

The fact remains, however, that many who initially become homeless against their will later gain a different perspective on it.

"I like the way my life is now."

This is what a tunnel-dweller told reporter Jennifer Toth. He goes on: "I'm independent and do what I want. It's not that I'm lazy or don't want to work. I walk all the way around the city most days to collect cans. This is the life I want." Another tunnel-dweller described being tracked down by a brother, who wanted to help him back to normal life. "He offered me $10,000. He just didn't understand. This is where I want to be for now. Maybe not forever, but for now."

One of David Wagner's subjects, escaping the constant battering of home, found that street life "was cool. I slept where I wanted. I hung out with people, I drank. I was free as a bird." According to another, who fled an abusive home at age twelve, "it was fine. I traveled, went all the way down the coast, down South. It was great, and I was never turning back, no matter what happened."

Even when the street is just the least worst alternative, people often feel they have more support there than they had at home. One runaway, describing his street friends to Katherine Coleman Lundy, said, "If they need food, need a few dollars, I'll give 'em a few dollars. . . . Whenever I need something, if I need it, they got it, they'll give it to me." A runaway told Jennifer Toth, "We've got real support from each other, not for just an hour from some social worker, but from people who really care and understand."

What would come of it?

If we let the homeless find their own places of refuge and helped them habilitate those places (instead of rousting them wherever they settle), if we channeled to them the vast amounts of food that are discarded routinely every day (instead of forcing them to grovel for food at shelters), if we actively assisted them to support themselves on their own terms (instead of ours), just think—homelessness would largely cease to exist as "a problem." It would become something we're always working at in the cities, like street maintenance. The streets in our cities are never going to be "fixed." They're going to be falling apart *forever*—and we're going to be fixing them forever. We don't think of street maintenance as "a problem," because it's something we've *acceded to*.

If we were to accede to homelessness, then we and the homeless would (for a change) be working together instead of at loggerheads. Keeping people sheltered, fed, and protected would become a common concern and a common task.

Acceding to homelessness doesn't mean that panhandlers, bag ladies, and street drunks are going to disappear—any more than maintaining the streets means that potholes, closed lanes, and traffic jams are going to disappear. Acceding to homelessness (like acceding to earthquakes) means dealing with reality, it doesn't mean doing away with it.

I'm not ENTIRELY alone!

Near the end of his landmark study of homelessness, *Checkerboard Square: Culture and Resistance in a Homeless Community*, David Wagner writes:

> What if homeless people . . . were offered the opportunity of collective mobility and collective resources *rather than individual scrutiny, surveillance, and treatment? What if the dense social networks and cohesive subcultures that constitute the homeless community were utilized by advocates, social workers, and others? What if housing could be provided near the geographic areas in which street groups congregate, decent housing that does not require leaving the group but that could be shared by street friends . . . What if social benefits were distributed not individually but collectively so that income maintenance or resources for food, shelter, and other goods were given to an entire group of people, not to individuals. That is, one would not need to wait for hours, provide all aspects of one's personal life, and come into a welfare office continually to be recertified, but would obtain a collective grant as part of a cohort of homeless people (or other group of poor people).*

All these suggestions (which even Wagner concedes are radical) represent accedence to the realities of homelessness. They're designed to help the homeless live decently *while* homeless—and to live the way they *want* to live (as opposed to the way government caretakers think they *should* live).

Objections

The idea of acceding to homelessness will raise objections on all sides. Liberals will perceive it as "giving up" on the homeless, but this would be like saying that acceding to street decay means giving up on the streets. Acceding to homelessness means listening to the poor, who believe they can take care of themselves—with the help they want instead of the help the respectably housed think they "should" have.

At the other end of the political spectrum, conservatives will perceive acceding to homelessness as coddling freeloaders, who should be disciplined and punished until they "get a job." Eventually they may see that it's like helping a poor fisherman get together some fishing tackle instead of giving him fish to eat.

Officialdom's objections will be the loudest, however, because its stake in homelessness goes beyond mere principles. Many people make their living "fighting" homelessness, and they'll see its disappearance as threatening their livelihood (though naturally they won't be silly enough to put it this way).

In 1998 Los Angeles, stealing a shopping cart would earn you a thousand-dollar fine and a hundred days behind bars. When an anonymous donor arranged to distribute a hundred "legal" shopping carts to the homeless, officials pulled a long face and denounced it as "well-intentioned but misguided."

The most telling objection of all

Acceding to homelessness—actually allowing the poor to make a living on the streets—would open the prison gates of our culture. The disenfranchised and disaffected would pour out. It would be the first great movement of people to that social and economic no man's land I call "beyond civilization."

The Tribe of Crow, no longer suppressed, would grow—perhaps explosively.

We wouldn't want that to happen, would we? Heavens to Betsy, no.

It would be chaotic. It might even be exciting.

Carlos, a runaway living under a loose grate in Manhattan's Riverside Park, told Jennifer Toth: "I'd change the world so there would be a place for us. A good place where we would have real freedom and not live in a hole."

Some dangerous ideas here . . . a place for the homeless . . . a good place . . . real freedom . . . not in a hole . . .

Put more guards on the walls. Reinforce the gates.

PART SIX

The New Tribal Revolution

You never change things by fighting the existing reality.
To change something, build a new model that makes the
existing model obsolete.

BUCKMINSTER FULLER

The tracks of our ancestors have been wiped away by the
Great Forgetting. It's not up to us to replant their exact
footprints, but to make our own, equally original tracks.

CARL COLE, AGE NINETEEN

The Tribe of Crow—and others

Thanks to his father, Jeffrey was able to live as a vagabond without ever being stigmatized as homeless. He clearly had no interest in working, but no one ever sneered "Get a job!" at him, because he never needed to stick out his hand for alms. He may have been too lucky for his own good, for had he been truly homeless, he might have found his true place in the world as a member of the Tribe of Crow.

But of course this tribe isn't for everyone.

When I first described the New Tribal Revolution in *My Ishmael*, I was rather like an astronomer describing a planet whose existence has been deduced but which has yet to be seen by any eye. If asked, I couldn't have furnished a single example of what I was talking about. Only after a year of vague groping did it occur to me that the circus (which I'd used as another sort of model in *Providence: The Story of a Fifty-Year Vision Quest*) is in fact organized in a way that is authentically tribal. (And I subsequently added this example to later editions of *My Ishmael*.)

But even so: only a single example?

After more months of vague groping, I realized I was preoccupied by the ethnic tribal model, designed to make a group of sixty or seventy individuals totally self-sufficient. I was looking at size and structure and forgetting benefits.

The *East Mountain News*

As soon as I began looking at the problem in a different way, I realized that Rennie and I and two other people had once (quite unconsciously) made our living in an authentically tribal way producing the *East Mountain News* in a vast area east of Albuquerque, New Mexico. Rennie and I started the paper as a speculative venture with virtually no capital. After putting out a couple of issues we got a call from Hap Veerkamp, an old newspaper man living in forced retirement (because no one would hire him at his age). He said he could do literally anything on a newspaper—except sell advertising. We said we'd love to have his stories and pictures, but if we didn't find people who could sell advertising we were going to be out of business very soon. He said he'd give it a shot. A few weeks later we heard from C.J. Harper, a young woman who wanted desperately to be a writer and who had an idea for a column that we might like. We liked the column and we liked her. The next question was, "Can you sell advertising?"

She said, "I can sell anything."

Why it worked

Suddenly we were in business—in a modest way. None of us was salaried. At the end of the week, when the issue was out, Rennie would sit down with C.J. and Hap and divvy up the advertising revenue that was left over from paying the printing bill. It was our rule only to print as much newspaper in any week as could be paid for out of advertising revenue. If we had enough advertising for twelve pages, we printed twelve, and that was "a good week." If we had only enough for eight pages, we printed eight, and that was "a fair week."

The newspaper worked for us for two reasons. First, we all enjoyed a very low standard of living, so what we got from the paper (a pittance by normal standards) was enough. Second, it wasn't just a way of making money. We all loved the paper and were intensely proud of our contributions to it. Hap's photos were as good as any published in any big-city paper. C.J.'s columns were fabulous. Rennie's features and news stories could have served as journalism-school models. Still slogging away at the sixth version of the book that would someday be a novel called *Ishmael*, I gave only three days a week to the paper, doing design and typesetting, but it gave me a break from writing and a chance to do other things I enjoy.

We were nothing like the size of an ethnic tribe, nor were we living in community, but we were nonetheless receiving the chief benefits of tribal life.

The *East Mountain News* as circus

As at the circus, each of us had a job to do that was essential to the success of the whole. As at the circus, the worst job was the boss's (and that was held by Rennie); no one envied her or dreamed for a moment that she was overpaid.

Just as at the circus, everyone knew the paper had to make money, but making money wasn't the object. Like circus folks, we had a way of making a living that suited us. To keep that, we had to keep the paper going. We all *needed* the paper.

Without discussing it, we all knew that, like a circus, we had to keep the paper going so the paper could keep *us* going. The only trouble was, the tribe needed a couple members more, and we didn't quite see this. The boss needed to share some of her more exhausting tasks—and there were plenty of those, considering that we were covering an area the size of Rhode Island. Rennie was being progressively worn out, but the people we needed didn't present themselves to throw in their lot with ours and (at the same time) to extend our business so that they too could make their living from it. Several people presented themselves to be *hired,* but they were only interested in the wage. When they saw how little they'd be making, they walked away. They weren't content to live out of the paper and make its success their own, as the rest of us were doing.

The success and failure of the paper

The startling success of the paper was that, by building it tribally, Rennie and I were able to start a business with almost no capital (a very small amount of cash and some retired typesetting equipment generously contributed by Rennie's brother, James). It would have taken hundreds of thousands of dollars to build a paper in the ordinary way, staffing it entirely with personnel hired at normal wages. Built in the ordinary way, it might have taken five or more years for the paper to break even. Built tribally, it broke even the first week. Given the huge area to be covered and its relatively small advertising base, the paper would never have generated enough profit to appeal to a publisher with ordinary capitalistic goals. And in fact, after we sold it (to a local real estate broker who intended to run it just as a business), it failed very quickly.

Realistically speaking, the area at that time couldn't support a newspaper as a capitalistic venture. What it could have supported was a shopper (an advertising sheet with a few token stories). And in fact, after the *East Mountain News* folded, its place was taken by a shopper.

The tribal benefit

The Albuquerque paper didn't cover the news on "our side" of the mountain at all, except for the occasional homicide. For the first time ever, because of the *East Mountain News,* people were able to find out what was going on in their area—school events, political events, social events—the whole spectrum of life that counts as "news." Though they had no way of knowing it, this was a direct benefit of our willingness to build the paper tribally. Building in the ordinary way, we couldn't have *afforded* to offer a real newspaper.

I wasn't personally invested in making the *East Mountain News* a "real" newspaper. My end of the business was putting the ads together. Once, after a succession of four- and eight-page issues had left us all feeling pinched, I said, "Why don't we just do a shopper?" This was instantly voted down. Rennie, Hap, and C.J. were in it because it was a *newspaper,* not because it earned money. The fact that it would earn more money as a shopper was irrelevant to them. They would have ceased getting what they *wanted* if it had become a shopper, and just having more money wouldn't have compensated them for the loss.

The important thing to see is that we were not "giving up" something by being tribal. We were *getting* something by being tribal—something that would have been out of reach otherwise. We weren't tribal because we were noble and altruistic; we were tribal because we were greedy and selfish.

What happened to Hap and C.J.?

We used the paper as a means of providing a living for all of us. For example, when Hap needed a new tire, we traded the local tire company an ad for it. When C.J. couldn't get a phone on her own signature, we co-signed with her. We didn't doubt for a moment that, if our positions had been reversed, they would have done the same for us.

When we sold the paper, we strongly advised the new owner to keep on working with Hap and C.J., but he soon made it clear he had other ideas. Hap by this time had become something of a celebrity through his work on the paper, so he had no trouble getting a job on the Torrance Country *Citizen*, a paper whose area of coverage overlapped ours to the south. He's still there as of this writing. The picture of me that appears on the dust jacket of *Providence* was taken by him while we were revisiting the area in 1993.

C.J. got married, left the area, and has been out of touch ever since. If you see her, tell her we'd like to hear from her.

Tribal business: the ingredients

Merely being tribal is no guarantee of success, of course. The normal elements needed for success have to be there as well. In our case, there had to be a public need for a newspaper and a fairly large number of businesses looking for an advertising venue, and we had both those things.

But beyond that, Rennie and I were quite incredibly lucky in finding two people who were ready to throw in their lot with ours in building a newspaper, who were content to make a living out of it (as opposed to a killing), and who were used to living on very little (as we were ourselves). With all this, we could hardly miss.

I think what's needed at a minimum is a group of people (1) who, among them, have all the competencies needed to start and run a given business, (2) who are content with a modest standard of living, and (3) who are willing to "think tribally"— that is, to take what they need out of the business rather than to expect set wages.

What ventures lend themselves to it?

As far as I can see, any enterprise that can succeed in the conventional way can succeed in the tribal way—with a few exceptions. A business that's built around the work of a single individual doesn't seem to lend itself to a tribal approach. For example, it's hard to imagine an internist and his or her office staff working together tribally. The disparity between what the internist puts in and what everyone else puts in is just too great. On the other hand, a tribal hospital isn't inconceivable, for there the internist would be putting in the same amount as the surgeon, the administrator, the anesthesiologist, and so on. I haven't been able to figure out any way to make the author's business into a tribal one (unless s/he prefers to be self-published).

To mention just a few things, restaurants, lawn-care businesses, and construction businesses could all be done tribally (and I'm sure many already are). Keep in mind that, as previously defined, a tribe is nothing more than a coalition of people working together as equals to make a living. I really see no limit to the possibilities.

A new tribal venture

People often ask if I consider myself a Leaver. In the past I replied, "Certainly not. I'm a prisoner of the same Taker economic system as you are. I'm entirely dependent on the vast corporate machinery that publishes, distributes, and sells my books." I then added that I'd be very glad to *reduce my dependence* on this machinery, even by ten percent, for this would represent at least a ten percent liberation from the prison. But only recently have Rennie and I taken decisive steps to achieve that ten percent.

I produce a lot of material that has little or no "commercial" value (is not attractive to the corporate publishing machine), but this doesn't mean that it's of no interest to my readers. In order to make this material available to those who want it (and hopefully to win that ten-percent degree of freedom), we decided to start a company called New Tribal Ventures, which will make certain of my works available to the public *outside* the corporate machinery of U.S. publishing. For example, two short books called *The Book of the Damned* and *The Tales of Adam* contain some of the most powerful expressions of my ideas I've ever achieved, but everyone agrees they're not "commercial" properties. These will be offered by New Tribal Ventures as a two-volume set entitled *An Animist Testament*.

Tribal tasks and organizational patterns

In the neo-futurist company, all members of the tribe do everything—write, perform, sell tickets, clean up, and so on. The same is true in the Culpepper and Merriweather Great Combined Circus, where all do everything—set up the tent, take care of the animals, perform, and so on.

The *East Mountain News* was organized differently. Hap and C.J. gathered news and sold advertising. I assembled the ads and did the typesetting and copy-editing. Rennie assembled all the news, did the layout, and was responsible for a host of managerial chores—far too many chores, as it turned out. Since no one had presented himself or herself to assist in a tribal way, we needed to hire people to shoulder some of her burdens, but we weren't making enough money to do that.

We failed to see that one important chore was not being done by any one of us, a chore that might be called *marketing*. No one presented himself or herself to extend the living of the tribe by performing this function. As a result, through lack of business sense and expertise, we ended up running into a wall we couldn't get around. We needed to hire support for Rennie, but were unable to do so because we were missing a tribal member we didn't even know we were missing.

A self-sustaining tribe needs to perform *all* the functions that will make it successful. A tribe of cabinet makers is not going to suceed without a member who knows how to *sell* cabinets.

Cradle-to-grave security?

Undoubtedly the greatest benefit of the ethnic tribal life is that it provides its members cradle-to-grave security. As I must always begin by saying, this isn't the result of the saintliness or unselfishness of tribal peoples. Baboons, gorillas, and chimpanzees enjoy exactly the same sort of security in their social groups. Groups that provide such security are obviously going to hold onto their members much more readily than groups that don't. Once again, it's a matter of natural selection. A group that doesn't take good care of its members is a group that doesn't command much loyalty (and probably won't last long).

But will occupational tribes provide such security to their members? Not instantly, obviously. If you and your brother start a conventional business on Tuesday, he can hardly expect to retire on Wednesday with full salary for the rest of his life— though he may hope to do that in twenty years, if he helps to build the business during that time.

The fact that ethnic tribes can provide their members with cradle-to-grave security is a true measure of their wealth. The people of our culture are rich in gadgets, machines, and entertainment, but we're all too aware of the dreadful consequences of losing a job. For some people—all too many—it seems to spell the end of the world; they go "postal," pick up the nearest automatic weapon, open fire on their former bosses, and finish off with a bullet in their own brains. These are people who are definitely short on feelings of security.

What about care for the elderly?

I've been asked if "retired circus performers are cared for by young performers" the way the elderly are cared for in ethnic tribes. This isn't how circus life works—but it also isn't how ethnic tribal life works. Old hunters aren't "cared for" by young hunters.

To begin with, a circus isn't just performers. Performers are vastly outnumbered by people who do all sorts of things, just as the actors you see on a movie screen are vastly outnumbered by the people involved in putting that image on the screen. Next, to talk about "retired circus performers" doesn't reflect the reality of circus life—or the reality of life in an ethnic tribe, where there's no such thing as a "retired hunter." When performers can no longer perform, they move on to other jobs in the circus. They don't need to be "cared for" just because they're no longer working the high wire or performing acrobatics.

What's your model of "care" for the elderly? If it includes all the services of a state-of-the-art hospital, then obviously no tribe is going to provide such a thing. IBM and General Motors don't run hospitals for the use of their employees; they offer them health insurance, which any tribe is free to do as well.

If your model of "care" for the elderly includes food, clothing, shelter, and the same sort of attention that elderly people in ethnic tribes receive, then this is perfectly well within the scope of an occupational tribe.

Tribes of the mind

People tend to imagine occupational tribes in a sort of postapocalyptic fantasy world. They're startled when I point out that they can have health insurance and retirement plans (if they want them) or that the government is going to be just as interested in collecting their taxes and social security payments as anyone else's. But if that's the case, they then ask, what's the point of what we're doing? If the world is just going to go on as before, why bother? These are questions that can't be answered often enough.

Mother Culture teaches that a *savior* is what we need—some giant St. Arnold Schwarzenegger who is a sort of combination of Jesus, Jefferson, Dalai Lama, Pope, Gandhi, Gorbachev, Napoleon, Hitler, and Stalin all rolled into one. The other six billion of us, according to Mother Culture, are helpless to do anything. We must simply wait quietly until St. Arnold arrives.

Daniel Quinn teaches that *no* single person is going to save the world. Rather (if it's saved at all), it will be saved by millions (and ultimately billions) of us *living a new way*. A thousand living a new way won't cause the dominant world order to topple. But that thousand will inspire a hundred thousand, who will inspire a million, who will inspire a billion—and *then* that world order will begin to look shaky!

(Next someone will ask, "But if the dominant world order gets shaky, what about my health insurance?")

The tribe IS its members

In a famous interchange at Columbia University, a faculty member who asserted that the faculty *is* the university was immediately told by the president of the university (former U.S. president Dwight D. Eisenhower) that the faculty are *employees* of the university. Mr. Eisenhower isn't on hand to contradict me when I say that the members of the tribe aren't employees of the tribe, they *are* the tribe. Indeed, that's the whole difference.

Because the tribe *is* its members, the tribe is what its members *want* it to be—nothing more and nothing less. If the members of your tribe expect it to provide exactly the sort of cradle-to-grave security that members of ethnic tribes enjoy, then make it so. But this isn't a requirement and may end up making little sense in a world of open tribes. In such a world, for example, it's perfectly conceivable that a husband and wife could belong to different occupational tribes—and that their children might want to belong to different tribes as well. Indeed, this openness to diversity is the whole point.

A tribe is a group of people making a living together, and there's no one right way for this to be done.

Be inventive.

Why make a living at all?

People sometimes react to my proposals as though there were something slightly distasteful and superfluous about the whole idea of "making a living"—tribally or otherwise. They seem to feel that if the New Tribal Revolution is all it's cracked up to be, then we shouldn't have to "make a living" at all, we should be able to live like the birds of the air.

Exactly so. That's the whole point, you might say.

Their misunderstanding isn't about the New Tribal Revolution; it's about the birds of the air. Sparrows may be "free as birds," but this doesn't mean they don't have to make a living. On the contrary, every living thing on earth has to do this. Gnats, geese, dolphins, chimpanzees, spiders, and frogs all have to expend energy to get what they need to stay alive. There is no creature that spends its life just lying there inert while needed resources flow in and do the work of keeping it alive. Even the green plants have a living to make. Each one is like a cottage industry, a regular little factory that takes energy from the sun and busily converts it into its own substance.

The tribe, in fact, is just a wonderfully efficient social organization that renders making a living easy for all—unlike civilization, which renders it easy for a privileged few and hard for the rest.

Another tribal example

The Neo-Futurists are an ensemble of artists who write, direct, and perform their own work dedicated to social, political, and personal enlightenment in the form of audience-interactive conceptual theater. (These words from the group's online Statement of Purpose.) Working in a "low/no tech poor theatre format," the group put together a unique postmodern dramatic endeavor that features an ever-changing collection of thirty plays performed in sixty minutes under the umbrella title *Too Much Light Makes the Baby Go Blind.* This signature work has (as of this writing) been running in Chicago since December 1, 1988, and had a successful run at the Joseph Papp Public Theater in New York City in 1993. In 1992 the Neo-Futurists opened their own Neo-Futurarium, boasting a 154-seat theater and an art gallery.

As many as thirteen members are active in the company at any one time, though the average performance tends to involve only eight or so. In addition to writing, directing, and performing *Too Much Light,* these thirteen perform virtually all chores associated with the theater and the production—manning the box office, cleaning up, recycling, producing the programs, buying the props, and so on.

Scuffling in the usual way

In a study of Gypsies and other itinerant peoples, anthropologist Sharon Bohn Gmelch lists some reasons these groups survive. They keep overhead low and have little interest in "material accumulation and capital expansion." They're willing to "exploit 'marginal' opportunities," to "fill gaps" in the economy, and to "accept a narrow profit margin from multiple sources." In short, they're experienced scufflers, as were all the residents of Madrid when we lived there—and as were all the members of the *East Mountain News,* none of whom made one hundred percent of his or her living from the newspaper.

The same is true of The Neo-Futurists. Though their goal is to make a living from the theater, most were probably deriving only twenty to fifty percent of their income from it in 1998, according to founder Greg Allen (who supplements his income by teaching theater history at Columbia College). Others have part-time jobs as massage therapist, physical trainer, CD-ROM writer, ultrasound technician, astrologer, secretaries, traditional waiters, and one "honest-to-god rock star in a famous punk band."

One of the company, Geryll Robinson, writes: "I wish I could lead my life without supporting/being supported by corporate America. I can't. I engage in a number of odd and often messy activities that people give me money for . . . I visited Chicago. I saw *Too Much Light.* I wanted in. I moved here. I auditioned. Now they own me. My life is good. Very good."

But can't an X be a tribe?

This is a question I'm asked again and again—substituting various terms for X. For example, I've been asked if an already-established conventional business can be converted into a tribal one. Yes, possibly, but with difficulty, the main one being that most people involved in conventional businesses are there for a wage, period. Some, having climbed up the wage scale, wouldn't care to climb down. Just as these might not be happy having less than a wage, others might not be happy having more than a wage—they just want to do their work and go home. But of course nothing's impossible.

A student in my Houston seminar asked if a bunch of people couldn't just get together and live tribally, and make their living elsewhere, individually. Certainly, and this is fine, but this is a commune, not a tribe, precisely because they're not involved in making a living together.

But can't a tribe be a commune—and can't a commune be a tribe?

We need some background to get at these questions.

Communities and tribes: origins

Like Topsy, most of the communities we inhabit just "grow'd," without mother or father, as it were. Once upon a time a century ago—or two or five—a general store was joined by a feed store, a butcher, a livery stable, a smithy, a tavern, and these were soon joined by a bank, a dry goods shop, a boarding house, a lawyer, a barber, a doctor, and so on. At some point or other, all realized they had a stake in the community's success—and in each other's success to a certain degree. The banker certainly wanted some grocer to succeed, but he didn't care whether it was Smith or Jones. The owner of the boarding house wanted some barber to succeed, but she didn't care whether it was Anderson or Adams.

Communes never begin in this haphazard way. They're "intentional" communities, originating among people who want to live together in pursuit of common ideals, usually in relative isolation. Communes are about living together and may or may not involve working together.

Tribes (and I speak here of "new" tribes, of course) originate among people who want to pool their energies and skills to make a living together. Tribes are about working together and may or may not involve living together.

Communities and tribes: membership

To the extent allowed by law and custom, ordinary communities make it their policy to exclude certain kinds of people and include all the rest. In other words, unless you belong to some abhorred race, religion, social class, or ethnic group, you're welcome to move in.

Communes proceed in the opposite way. Their policy is to include certain kinds of people and exclude all the rest. In other words, unless you subscribe to the group's special values (social, political, or religious), you're *not* welcome to move in. The tribal rule of thumb is: *Can you extend the living to include yourself?* In other words, if you want to live out of the tribal occupation, you'll have to extend the group's earning power to the point where it covers you. This is exactly what Hap and C.J. did for the *East Mountain News*. We couldn't have included them in the business if they hadn't extended it by selling advertising.

Can't a tribe be a commune?

As I said above, tribes are about working together and may or may not involve living together. But tribal people can live together without becoming a commune. Speaking of artisan, trader, and entertainer minorities such as Gypsies, Norwegian Taters, Irish Travelers, and the Nandiwalla of India, anthropologist Sharon Bohn Gmelch notes specifically that the social organization of these groups is flexible and "at its core, noncommunal."

The difficulty I see with a tribe becoming a commune is that communes traditionally choose their members on the basis of shared ideals. Shared ideals aren't irrelevant to tribal applicants, but they're overridden by the question "Can you extend our livelihood to include yourself?"

I can certainly say that it didn't occur to any of us on the *East Mountain News* that we should "start a commune." The idea would have struck us as ludicrous.

The tribe isn't about *living* together but about *making a living* together.

Can't a commune be a tribe?

The answer is, "Yes, a commune can definitely be a tribe; it's just a problematical way to begin."

Communes generally start with people who want to "get away from it all." Separating themselves from a corrupt, materialistic, and unjust society, they typically want to live "close to nature" alongside people with similar ideals. Because they intend to live simply, making a living seems almost incidental. They may farm, produce craft goods, or commute to ordinary jobs. As time goes on, all may work out exactly as planned—or it may not. Rustic simplicity may be less charming than expected. Perhaps some become bored with the work. Nerves fray, ideals are forgotten, friendships dissolve, and the thing is soon over. Or it may take a different direction. The members may refocus their attention from ideals to making a living together in a way that's more satisfactory. Remember, however, that this group originally came together on an entirely different basis, so it will be luck rather than design if they actually have some occupational interests and skills in common.

It's rather like going shopping for groceries that start with the letter *m*—mustard, mango, mackerel, mayonnaise, macaroni, and so on—and then later wondering if you happen to have the ingredients for *Cassoulet du Chef Toulousian*. It could happen, of course, but it's not as likely as if you'd gone shopping for those ingredients in the first place.

"Let's do the show right here in the barn!"

In cinematic legend this catch phrase springs to Mickey Rooney's lips in half a dozen movies he made with Judy Garland in the 1940s. Whether it was ever uttered in any film, its meaning is clear. Everyone understands that it emanates from a troupe of young entertainers looking for a chance to show off their talents.

It's important to note that it doesn't emanate from a group of people trying to *invent* something they might do together. In fact, they're a group because they *already know* what they can do together. Show business brought them together in the same way that the newspaper business brought us together with Hap and C.J. We might have been the best of friends, but only the newspaper could have pulled us together into a tribe. If we'd made up our minds to open an antique store or a computer software business, Hap and C.J. would never have been involved, no matter how close to them we might have been.

I say all this in answer to a question that must be in the back of many minds: Can't a bunch of miscellaneous friends become a tribe? The answer is yes, just the way a commune can become a tribe. It's perfectly possible, it's just not very likely—unless that bunch of friends was drawn together in the first place by a common occupational focus (as were the Neo-Futurists).

Aren't the Amish a farming tribe?

The Amish are a religious sect, an offshoot of the Mennonites. Here's what makes them communal rather than tribal: If you apply for membership, they'll be much more interested in your religious beliefs and your moral character than in your agricultural ambitions.

A commune "can be" a tribe, just as a lighthouse "can be" a grain silo and a prom gown "can be" a nurse's uniform. But the fact remains that we give things different names because we perceive them as different things. In Colonial New England, the settlers started communes, not tribes, and they knew the difference. Tribes were for savages and communes were for civilized people.

People will also ask, "Isn't Ben & Jerry's a tribal business?" And the answer is, Ben & Jerry's was a tribal business when Ben and Jerry were the company's only employees, personally making ice cream in a four-and-a-half-gallon freezer and scooping it up for customers in a remodeled gas station in Burlington, Vermont. After that point, their business grew not by adding members to their tribe but by adding employees in the conventional way. Ben & Jerry's isn't a tribal business, it's a values-led business (which doesn't make it any less admirable). Can a values-led business be a tribal business? Of course. It just isn't *automatically* a tribal business.

It's not my intention (or within my power) to divest the word *tribe* of its ordinary meanings. Rather it's my intention to invest it with a special one when used in the context of the New Tribal Revolution.

Noble savages?

While considering what it would take to start a health-care tribe, a physician mentioned the fact that medical professionals in our society generally have a pretty high standard of living—clearly implying that she perceived this to be some sort of obstacle or problem. A few questions revealed that she was unconsciously picturing the members of her health-care tribe as noble savages—too noble to charge for their services (and therefore unable to maintain the standard of living they're used to).

It's hard to know how to cope with this familiar bipolarity, which sees people as incapable of being anything but either totally selfish or totally altruistic. Like an on/off switch, they can only flop from one pole to the other. Tribal life functions in between these poles, and a tribe of totally altruistic individuals will fail as surely as a tribe of totally selfish individuals.

If a physician decided s/he would rather have a general practice in a small town than a specialized practice in a big city, would s/he expect to work for nothing? Of course not. People in small towns expect to pay for medical services. If a physician decides s/he would rather belong to a health-care tribe than to a conventional hospital, why would s/he expect to work for nothing? People know that physicians, whether they work in tribes or in hospitals, have to make a living just like everyone else.

D A N I E L   Q U I N N

An intermittent tribal business

As the 1973 film *The Sting* opens, we follow a pair of grifters, Johnny Hooker (Robert Redford) and Luther Coleman (Robert Earl Jones), as they work a short con known as the Jamaican Handkerchief on a man who, unbeknownst to them, is carrying money to mob boss Doyle Lonnegan (Robert Shaw). When Lonnegan learns of the con, he has Coleman murdered. To avenge his partner, Hooker decides to take Lonnegan for a really big score. As he sets this in train, we see that he belongs to a whole tribe of grifters, who generally make their living in straight jobs (for example as clerks or bank tellers) but who are always ready to come together as a tribe in one of the classic "big cons." A striking point is made of their readiness. When the single, wordless signal is given, they instantly abandon their jobs. Without asking how big the score will be or what their share is, they come together smoothly to assemble an elaborate theatrical production called a "big store." As in the circus, each member is supremely important when his or her moment comes. One studies Lonnegan to discover how to lure him into the con. Others work on sets, on costumes, on props. Though Henry Gondorff (Paul Newman) is clearly the boss, this doesn't make him uniquely important. All the jobs *must* be done—and the boss's is just one of them. In hierarchal organizations, the boss is a supreme being. In tribal organizations, the boss is just another worker. (This is exactly the way it was on the *East Mountain News.*)

My next tribal enterprise

Long before I identified the concept as tribal, I wanted to open a circus of learning such as I described in *Providence* and *My Ishmael*. Now I have a better idea of how to make this work in reality. Houston appeals to me because it isn't zoned, making it a crazy quilt of residential and commercial districts, and no one fusses if you run a business from your home. This makes it an ideal site for a learning circus, which combines spaces for working, exhibition, and performance to provide a center for work, play, performance, and education, involving (as teachers, performers, and participants) acrobats, jugglers, clowns, dancers, musicians, actors, set designers, magicians, lighting technicians, film makers, writers, potters, painters, sculptors, photographers, weavers, costumers, carpenters, electricians, and so on. No grades, no required courses, no tests—just learn all you want, whenever you want. Although open to all-age learners, it would make a marvelous resource for parents homeschooling their children, an option becoming more and more popular everywhere, with good reason. (Please note, however, that this isn't a "community learning center" for "student-directed learning." These are fine things, but I'm aiming at entertainment, not civic good works.) Someone asked why students would prefer this learning circus over a university. The two aren't competitive, and the strictly career-minded will surely prefer the more conventional of the two.

No timetable exists for this grand enterprise.

To distinguish is to know

It's important for me to point out (before others do) that I didn't invent tribal businesses; I just distinguished them from conventional ones and so made them especially visible. Now that you know what they are, you'll probably see them everywhere. In discussion with my seminar, Rennie brought to mind one we know in Portland, Oregon, the Rimskykorsakoffeehouse. This quirky local landmark, the creation of quirky local celebrity Goody Cable, almost has to be experienced to be believed. To take a table is to enter a special world that can really only be adequately described as tribal. When things get especially busy, customers will often be pressed into service to wait tables, and I know of one local author who waits tables one night a week just for the privilege of belonging to the tribe. There are often long lines of people waiting to get in; they like being there because the people working there obviously *like* being there.

Tribal people get more out of life.

Just think. It's taken me thirty thousand words to make those seven sound plausible.

The civilized hate and fear tribal people

People in traveling shows of every kind are viewed as exciting but dangerous people, people to be shunned when they're off-stage. This is part of their allure, especially for the young. In past ages Gypsies were constantly suspected of stealing children, probably because more than a few children in fact succumbed to the lure of Gypsy life. It's long been suspected that the tribalism of the Jews has contributed to their demonization. And certainly no effort has been spared on our part to destroy the tribalism of native peoples wherever we find them. Their tribalism is the very emblem of their "backwardness" and "savagery."

The civilized want people to be dependent on the prevalent hierarchy, not on each other. There's something inherently evil about people making themselves self-sufficient in small groups. This is why the homeless must be rousted wherever they collect. This is why the Branch Davidian community at Waco had to be destroyed; they'd never been charged with any crime, much less convicted—but they *had* to be doing something very, very nasty in there. The civilized want people to make their living individually, and they want them to live separately, behind locked doors—one family to a house, each house fully stocked with refrigerators, television sets, washing machines, and so on. That's the way *decent* folks live. Decent folks don't live in tribes, they live in communities.

Yet, oddly enough, as soon as you hold up the tribe as something desirable, decent folks will start insisting they're as tribal as any Bushman or Blackfoot.

Tribes and communities

Pressed into a hierarchal mold, the tribe becomes what the civilized call a community. Within the hierarchy of civilization in any age, community exhibits self-similarity at many different scales. The medieval Yorkshire village of Wharram Percy was a microcosm of feudal England, just as Evanston is a microcosm of modern America. This sort of fractal self-similarity between microcosm and macrocosm is, as John Briggs and David F. Peat point out, "a product of all the complex internal feedback relationships going on in a dynamical system" like our own. It's inevitable that Evanston—and East L.A. and Harlem and Broken Arrow, Oklahoma—are all going to reflect the hierarchal organization of our society as a whole, with rich folks here, middle-class folks here, and poor folks there. It doesn't matter that the rich of Evanston are better off than the rich of East L.A. or that the poor of Harlem are worse off than the poor of Broken Arrow. The *structure* is there.

The word *community* is itself an acknowledgment of decency and is withheld from the undeserving. Homosexuals struggled long and hard to become "the gay *community*," but pederasts and pornographers don't stand a chance. Hoodlums, criminals, convicts, and religious fanatics don't have communities, they have gangs, mobs, populations, and cults.

I can imagine totally decent people being attracted to Objectivism or Voluntary Simplicity or Creative Individualism. I have a harder time imagining them being attracted to the tribal life. Maybe it's just me.

A parable about sustainability

An inventor brought his plans for a new device to an engineer, who looked at them and said, "What you've got here is systemically flawed, which means it'll destroy itself after just a few minutes of operation."

"Not if it's well made," the inventor replied. "Every part must be made of the finest material and to very exact specifications."

The engineer had the device built, but it destroyed itself after just four minutes of operation. The inventor wasn't discouraged. "You didn't do what I told you," he said. "You've got to use much finer materials—the finest available—and make the parts to the most exact specifications."

The engineer tried again, and the new model worked for eight minutes. "You see?" said the inventor. "We're making tremendous progress. Try again, using even finer materials and more exact specifications." The new device lasted for ten minutes. The engineer was told to build yet another model, using still finer materials and still more exact specifications. The new model lasted for eleven minutes.

The inventor wanted to go on and on in this way, striving for perfect parts, but the engineer refused, saying, "Can't you see that our returns are diminishing here? It's a waste of time to try to make a dysfunctional design work by improving its parts. Bring me a viable design, and I'll guarantee you a device that'll work for years, using parts made from ordinary materials, to ordinary specifications."

Why what we've got is unsustainable

It's a fundamental tenet of our cultural mythology that the only thing wrong with us is that humans are not made well enough. We need to be made of finer materials, to some set of better specifications (provided, perhaps, by greened-up versions of our traditional religions). We just need to be made kinder, gentler, sweeter, more loving, less selfish, more far-sighted, and so on, then everything will be fine. Of course, no one succeeded in making us better last year or the year before that or the year before that or the year before that—or indeed any year in recorded history—but maybe *this* year we'll get lucky . . . or next year or the year after that.

What I've endeavored to say in all my books is that the flaw in our civilization isn't in the people, it's in the *system*. It's true that the system has been clanking along for ten thousand years, which is a long time in the timescale of an individual life, but when viewed in the timescale of human history, this episode isn't remarkable for its epic length but for its tragic brevity.

In *Ishmael* I compared our civilizational contraption to an aircraft that has been in the air for ten thousand years—but in free fall rather than in flight. If we stay with it, we'll crash with it, and soon. But if most of us lighten its load by abandoning it, it can probably stay in the air for a long time (while the rest of us try something that makes better sense).

Let's bail out and go over the wall!

Professor of anthropology James W. Fernandez writes, "Anthropologists, unlike philosophers, find that cultural worlds are brought into being by the performance (enactment) of *mixed metaphors.*" (Emphasis added.)

So there. I'm happy to mix a few metaphors in the cause of bringing into being a new cultural world.

After several hours spent discussing the movement beyond civilization to tribal living, one of the members of my seminar said he still couldn't see how it would serve to make human life more sustainable. We've come a ways since the last time I addressed this issue, so I should probably address it again here. It's a valid and important question. The New Tribal Revolution may give people a better life, but if it doesn't serve to perpetuate our species beyond a few decades, what's the point?

Right now there are about six billion of us in what I've called the culture of maximum harm. Only ten percent of these six billion are being maximally harmful—are gobbling up resources at top speed, contributing to global warming at top speed, and so on—but the other ninety percent, having nothing better in sight, want only to be like the ten percent. They envy that ten percent and are convinced that living in a way that is maximally harmful is the best way to live of all.

If we don't give them something better to want, we're doomed.

A systemic change

The New Tribal Revolution is an escape route from the prison of our culture. The walls of that prison are economic. That is, the need to make a living keeps us inside, because there's no way to make a living on the *other* side. We can't employ the Mayan Solution—we can't disappear into a life of ethnic tribalism. But we can disappear into a life of *occupational* tribalism.

Will this leave our civilization a smoking ruin? Certainly not. It will *diminish* it. As more and more people see that going over the wall means getting something better (not "giving up" something), more and more people will abandon the culture of maximum harm—and the more this culture is abandoned, the better. The escape route leads beyond civilization, beyond the thing that, according to our cultural mythology, is humanity's very last invention.

The escape route leads to humanity's *next* invention.

But even so, will this next invention give us a sustainable lifestyle? Here's how I assess this. Humans living in tribes was as ecologically stable as lions living in prides or baboons living in troops. The tribal life wasn't something humans sat down and figured out. It was the gift of natural selection, a proven success—not perfection but hard to improve on. Hierarchalism, on the other hand, has proven to be not merely imperfect but ultimately catastrophic for the earth and for us. When the plane's going down and someone offers you a parachute, you don't demand to see the warranty.

But why "humanity's" next great adventure?

In *The Story of B* and elsewhere I made a great point of establishing the fact that we—the Takers, the people of this culture—are *not* humanity, and I'll certainly never draw back from that statement. It isn't humanity that is presently converting this planet's biomass into human mass, it's the people of one culture—ours. It isn't humanity that is pressing thousands of species into extinction every year by its expansion, it's the people of one culture—ours.

Why then do I describe the New Tribal Revolution as "humanity's" next great adventure instead of "our" next great adventure? The answer is simple: civilization was not "our" adventure. As I've pointed out again and again in this book, civilization was an adventure that many peoples embarked upon. "We" weren't the only ones; we were just the only ones who stuck with it to the point of self-immolation. And if civilization wasn't just "our" great adventure, how could the *next* great adventure be just "ours"?

The New Tribal Revolution isn't intended to be ours alone— anyone can join who wants to, after all. But neither is it compulsory. The old tribalism with which humanity became humanity is as good as it ever was. It will never wear out or become obsolete. Landing on the moon was a great achievement for humanity, but that doesn't mean all humans have to do it.

PART SEVEN

Beyond Civilization

An important scientific innovation rarely makes its way by gradually winning over and converting its opponents. . . . What does happen is that its opponents gradually die out and that the growing generation is familiarized with the idea from the beginning.

MAX PLANCK

Liberation

During a period when millions were being liquidated as "enemies of the people," there was a certain "dangerous" poet who was famous for his uncanny ability to avoid Stalin's displeasure. A French journalist sought him out to ask if he'd been silenced under the latest reign of terror.

"Silenced!" the poet cried indignantly. "I declaim my poetry from the stage of the ———— Theater every Monday night!"

The journalist made a point of being there the following Monday, only to find the theater dark and locked. He hung around indecisively for a hour, then, as he was about to leave, a side door opened and the poet slipped out into the night.

"What happened?" the journalist asked him. "I thought you were going to read here tonight."

"I *did* read here tonight," the poet declared emphatically. "It just so happens that I'm at my best when reading before an empty house."

When people say my books have inspired them to "go someplace and start a commune," I have to wish them the best of luck—and bite back the impulse to tell them this is very far from anything I had in mind. If you can only be free living on a mountaintop or a desert island, then clearly you're something less than free.

Listening to the children

Whether by intention or not, suicides often reveal themselves in their choice of means. The guilty hang themselves. Sacrificial victims slash their throats. The discarded throw themselves off buildings or bridges. Tormented minds blow their brains out. Jeffrey in *My Ishmael* walked into a lake, telling us he'd failed to find his true element. He just couldn't get into his lungs the air others seem to breathe so easily.

I've talked about Jeffrey (or his real-life prototype, Paul Eppinger) to many audiences, always with the feeling that I haven't made my point, which is that he wasn't extraordinary. He's to be found everywhere among our children—if only we'll start listening. I don't just mean listening to their words—they may not have the words. Listen to the stories they tell with their gestures of profound alienation and despair, the stories of pandemic suicide, of drug use among younger and younger children every year, of mind-boggling acts of violence committed by round-faced teens against their families and friends. Listen to their words as well, of course, but never forget that they've been schooled to say what people want to hear; the mass murderers among them are almost always remembered as nice, polite youngsters.

I know I've failed to make myself understood when people tell me Jeffrey "should have gone to a commune." This idea represents a profound misunderstanding of where the space of our freedom is to be discovered.

The Littleton bloodbath

The previous page was written half a year before the mind-boggling act of violence committed on "Free Cookie Day," April 20, 1999, at Columbine High School in Littleton, Colorado, where fifteen died in half as many minutes. Even though the perpetrators of this massacre were two intensely unpopular boys, one classmate afterward managed to remember at least one of them as *nice*.

I was unpopular at my own high school—not quite as unpopular as those two, but I dealt with it the same way, by flouting it and even perversely cultivating it. I too had an accomplice, achieving some "solidarity in exclusion." Both of us resorted to violence on occasion, but of course we didn't dream of assassinating hundreds, dynamiting the school, and crashing an airplane into a city block.

Things were different then, almost half a century ago—not that they were "good old days." We were never allowed to forget that one wrong word or one insane moment could trigger a nuclear holocaust that would leave our world a smoking ruin. But if that didn't happen, we two faced a future of literally unlimited promise. No one had as yet realized we were in the process of making the earth uninhabitable. No one had as yet doubted that we could go on living exactly this way *forever*. So we had *hope*—bushels, acres, and tons of hope. We had a way to go that we *knew* would work. We had *choices*. We didn't doubt for a moment that we could do *anything* we really wanted to do, because everything was just going to go on exactly *this* way, getting better and better and better and better and better and better and better and better and better and better and better . . . forever.

Listening to the monsters

Would Eric Harris and Dylan Klebold have become "the monsters next door" (as *Time* magazine dubbed them) if they'd had another way to go? At school they were harassed as "dirtbags" and "faggots" and pummeled with bottles and rocks thrown from classmates' passing cars. Did they go there because they *wanted* this abuse? No, we understand perfectly well why they went there: they had no choice in the matter. They "had" to go, compelled by law and social pressure. If they'd had another way to go, they would have disappeared from Columbine long before their only dream became a dream of vengeance and suicide.

Would brain scans have revealed they were "genetically inclined to violence?" Perhaps so, and so what? A brain scan might reveal the same about me. Remind me to tell you about the time I came within a split second of killing a man with my bare hands, a catastrophe only averted by the narrowest margin of good luck for us both. Being "genetically inclined to violence" doesn't doom you to becoming a mass murderer—but having no hope may do just that. Frankenstein's creature only became a monster when he saw he could never be anything else.

It's estimated that, since the days of my youth, depression among children has increased by 1000% and teen suicide by 300%. Since 1997, classroom-assassins have killed two in Mississippi, three in Kentucky, five in Arkansas, and thirteen in Colorado. Make a graph of these numbers and watch them go exponential in years to come—unless we start giving our kids a new way to go and some real hope for the future.

A cultural space of our own

People who are reluctant to spend their lives building some pharaoh's pyramid all have a common need, but the need is felt most acutely by the young, who are the real pack-animals of the operation. Sixty years ago raw graduates took jobs in factories, where they could at least expect to climb the same ladder of advancement as their parents. In the postindustrial age young people (as James E. Côté and Anton L. Allahar point out) are becoming increasingly ghettoized in retail and service sectors, where they endlessly lift and carry, stock shelves, push brooms, bag groceries, and flip burgers, gaining no skills and seeing no path of advancement ahead of them.

For them and for us, it isn't geographical space we want, it's cultural space. Carlos, who made his home under a grate in Riverside Park, knew that a certain kind of freedom comes with living in a hole. But he also knew it isn't "real freedom" if you have to live in a hole to get it. He wanted the kind of freedom people have when they live where they please and don't have to resort to a hole, even in "the scenic Ozarks" or "the foothills of Kentucky." He wanted a whole world's worth of freedom—and so do most of us, I think. To get that, we'll have to take the world back from the pharaohs. It won't be hard. They're not expecting it—but even if they were, they'd be helpless to stop it.

Why things didn't end up a-changin'

Lots of songs about revolution came out during the hippie era of the 1960s and 1970s, but the revolution itself never materialized, because it didn't occur to the revolutionaries that they had to come up with a revolutionary way of *making a living*. Their signature contribution was starting communes—a hot new idea from the same folks who gave us powdered wigs.

When the money ran out and parents got fed up, the kids looked around and saw nothing to do but line up for jobs at the quarries. Before long, they were dragging stones up to the same pyramids their parents and grandparents and great-grandparents had been working on for centuries.

This time it'll be different. It'd better be.

Another story to be in

As developed in *Ishmael,* the "story" we're enacting in our culture is this: *The world was made for Man to conquer and rule, and Man was made to conquer and rule it; and under Man's rule, the world might have become a paradise except for the fact that he's fundamentally and irremediably flawed.* This story—itself mythology—is the foundation for all our cultural mythology, and I said in *Ishmael* that it isn't possible for people simply to give up living in such a story. They must have *another story to be in.*

It didn't occur to me when I wrote these words that people might imagine this "other" story to be a brand-new fabrication that I or some panel of mythologists was going to sit down and conjure up out of nothing, but of course a few did. But oddly enough, when challenged to articulate this other story, which I'd described as having been enacted here during the first three million years of human life, I found I couldn't do it in any very convincing fashion. This was because I was trying to formulate it in a way that was parallel to ours, point by point. I failed to realize for a good long time that the other story was much simpler (much more "primitive") than ours—and that I'd *already* articulated it. To my mind it's the most beautiful story ever told.

There is no one right way for people to live.

No one right way

Once you recognize it, it's perfectly clear that this is the story that was enacted here during the first three or four million years of human life. Of course, there's a clear sense in which ours is just a special case of a much wider story, written in the living community itself from the beginning, some five billion years ago: *There is no one right way for ANYTHING to live.*

No one right way to hinge a jaw.
No one right way to build a nest.
No one right way to design an eye.
No one right way to move underwater.
No one right way to breed.
No one right way to bear young.
No one right way to shape a wing.
No one right way to attack your prey.
No one right way to defend yourself against attack.

This is how we humans got from there to here, by enacting this story, and it worked sensationally well until about ten thousand years ago, when one *very* odd culture sprang into being obsessed with the notion that there must be a single right way for people to live—and indeed a single right way to do almost anything.

Gotcha this way!

But these words will hardly be taken in before some wiseacre thinks to ask: "But aren't you saying, Mr. Quinn, that *the tribal way* is the right way for people to live?"

I'm saying nothing of the kind. As I noted above, the gifts of natural selection aren't perfect (much less "right"), but they're damned hard to improve on. The tribal way isn't the right way, it's just a way that worked for millions of years, in contrast to the hierarchal way, which has brought us face to face with extinction after a mere ten thousand years.

For all I know, the tribal way may in the future be superceded by some other way that works better for us in circumstances that are obviously going to be very different from those of the past. In fact, isn't that exactly what I'm proposing in these pages? After all, I'm not suggesting we return to the tribal way as it was known here during the first three million years of human life—or as it's still known among surviving aboriginal peoples. Old-style ethnic tribalism is, for the foreseeable future, utterly out of reach for us.

The tribalism of the New Tribal Revolution isn't proposed as an end—as something *right* and to be clung to at any cost—it's proposed as a beginning, at a time when we must either make a new beginning or reconcile ourselves to joining the dinosaurs in the very near future.

Gotcha that way!

Someone else will try this: "But aren't you in fact saying, Mr. Quinn, that having no one right way to live is *the one right way to live?*"

No, I'm not saying that, because that's just meaningless babble. Having no one right way to live is *not* a way to live, any more than having no one right way to cook an egg is a way to cook an egg.

Knowing that there's no one right way to live won't tell you how to live, any more than knowing that there's no one right time to go to bed will tell you when to go to bed.

The beginning is not the end

Beyond civilization isn't a geographical space up in the mountains or on some remote desert isle. It's a cultural space that opens up among people with new minds.

Old minds think:	New minds think:
How do we solve these problems?	*How do we make happen what we want to happen?*

As you discuss the ideas found in this book with your friends, you'll be able to spot the old minds easily. They're the ones who are always "playing the devil's advocate," always proposing and concentrating on difficulties, always nailing the progress of your dialogue down to problems. Focus instead on what you want to happen and how to make it happen, rather than on all the things that might keep it from happening.

Believe it or not, a real person once said to me, "Yes, but won't we still have to pay taxes?" Yes, and you'll still have to curb your dog and observe the speed limit and shovel your sidewalks when it snows. And it will still be a good idea to get to the airport a few minutes before your flight leaves.

What, no miracles?

Jack and Jill spent some days with their friend Simon on his small sailboat. One morning they woke up to find the boat was sinking.

"What in the world are we going to do?" Jill asked.

"Don't worry," said Jack, "Simon's very ingenious."

Simon called to them, "Come on, we've got to abandon ship."

Jill was alarmed, but Jack reassured her that Simon wouldn't let them down.

"We're only a hundred yards from shore," Simon said. "Let's go!"

"But how are we going to save ourselves?" the couple wanted to know.

"We're going to swim for it, of course!" Seeing Jack's look of disappointment, Simon asked him what was wrong.

Jack said, "I was hoping you could find a way of translating us directly ashore, *without our having to get wet.*"

An early reader expressed the same disappointment with me. He was hoping I'd be able to find a way of translating us directly to our new economic homeland without our having to "get wet" in the Taker economy that surrounds us. The ultimate New Tribal economy (which at best I can only dimly imagine) is the dry land ahead. To reach it while holding ourselves disdainfully aloof from the economy around us would make walking on water seem like a very minor miracle indeed.

140 words of advice

You don't have to have all the answers. Certainly I don't have them. It's always better to say "I don't know" than to fake it and get into hot water.

Make people formulate their own questions. Don't take on the responsibility of figuring out what their difficulty is.

Never try to answer a question you don't understand. Make the askers explain it; keep on insisting until it's clear, and nine times out of ten they'll supply the answer themselves.

People will listen when they're ready to listen and not before. Probably, once upon a time, *you* weren't ready to listen. Let people come to it in their own time. Nagging or bullying will only alienate them.

Don't waste time with people who want to argue. They'll keep you immobilized forever. Look for people who are *already* open to something new.

A dynamite ending

Like any author, I figured that, when the time came, I'd have a dynamite ending for this book—a great clash of cymbals, a ray of pure sunshine knifing through the clouds (you know), but nothing like that presented itself. I mentioned this to Rennie yesterday afternoon, just as a matter of interest. I wasn't expecting her to work on the problem, because it didn't occur to me it *was* a problem. All the same, at three in the morning, she woke me up to explain why no terrific ending had presented itself and why no terrific ending was *going* to present itself. While she was at it, she told me I should include Hap and C.J. in the dedication and that this was the first of my books she actually *wanted* to have dedicated to her (the other dedications she more or less just put up with).

There's no ending in this book at all, she told me, because it's all one hundred percent *beginning,* and of course she's right.

But this just means no dynamite ending is going to turn up *here.* The dynamite ending is on the other side of this page and on out past the cover, where the actual revolution is going to take place.

The dynamite ending is for *you* to write.

Bibliography

Anderson, Ray C. *Mid-Course Correction: Toward a Sustainable Enterprise: The Interface Model.* Atlanta: Peregrinzilla Press, 1998.

Associated Press. "Brother in Custody for Alabama Death," June 19, 1998.

———. "Child Charged with Attempted Murder," February 21, 1998.

———. "Recent U.S. School Shootings," May 21, 1998.

———. "Homeless Given New Carts in L.A.," July 15, 1998.

———. "Berkeley Cracks Down on Homeless," November 26, 1998.

Attali, Jacques. *Millennium: Winners and Losers in the Coming World Order.* New York: Random House, 1991.

Baltrusch, Libby S. *The New Age Community Guidebook: Alternative Choices in Lifestyles.* 4th Ed. Middletown, Calif.: Harbin Springs, 1989.

Bass, Dina. "Poll Finds Sharp Rise in Drug Use Among Youngsters." *Los Angeles Times*, August 14, 1997.

Briggs, John, and David F. Peat. *Seven Life Lessons of Chaos: Spiritual Wisdom from the Science of Change.* New York: HarperCollins, 1999.

Brokaw, Chet. "South Dakota Suicides Worry Officials." Associated Press, March 14, 1998.

Cooper, Diana Starr. *Night After Night.* Washington, D.C.: Island Press, 1994.

Côté, James E., and Anton L. Allahar. *Generation on Hold: Coming of Age in the Late Twentieth Century.* New York: New York University Press, 1996.

Culhane, John. *The American Circus: An Illustrated History.* New York: Henry Holt, 1990.

Dawkins, Richard. *The Selfish Gene.* Oxford: Oxford University Press, 1989.

Eppinger, Paul, and Charles Eppinger. *Restless Minds, Quiet Thoughts: A Personal Journal.* Ashland, Or.: White Cloud Press, 1994.

Feldman, S. Shirley, Glen R. Elliot, eds. *At the Threshold: The Developing Adolescent.* Cambridge: Harvard University Press, 1990.

Fernandez, James W., ed. *Beyond Metaphor: The Theory of Tropes in Anthropology.* Stanford: Stanford University Press, 1991.

Gibbs, Nancy. "The Littleton Massacre." *Time,* May 5, 1999.

Gmelch, Sharon Bohn. "Groups That Don't Want In: Gypsies and Other Artisan, Trader, and Entertainer Minorities." *Annual Review of Anthropology* 15 (1986): 307–330.

Gorbachev, Mikhail. *The Search for a New Beginning: Developing a New Civilization.* San Francisco: Harper San Francisco, 1995.

Gore, Al. *Earth in the Balance: Ecology and the Human Spirit.* New York: Houghton Mifflin, 1992.

Greenberg, Josh. "Teen Drug Use Has Doubled in 4 Years, U.S. Says." *Los Angeles Times,* August 21, 1996.

Grossman, Ron. "The Smallest Show on Earth: Tiny Troupe Surviving in the Hamlets." *Chicago Tribune,* July 10, 1986.

Irvine, Martha. "Chicago's Homeless Face 'Eviction.'" The Associated Press, January 29, 1999.

Killion, Thomas W., ed. *Gardens of Prehistory: The Archaeology of Settlement Agriculture in Greater Mesoamerica.* Tuscaloosa: The University of Alabama Press, 1992.

Kim, Eun-Kyung. "Survey Shows Teen Drug Use Rose." Associated Press, August 21, 1998.

Knutson, Lawrence L. "Report Cites Harassment of Homeless." Associated Press, January 6, 1999.

Kritzer, Jamie. "Teens at Risk: Survey Results Indicate That Young People Are Using Illegal Drugs in Greater Numbers Than Before." *Montgomery Advertiser*, September 22, 1996.

Lee, Richard B., Irven DeVore, eds. *Man the Hunter*. Chicago: Aldine Publishing Company, 1968.

Lloyd, Leslie. "Six Plead Guilty to Killing Family." Associated Press, February 21, 1998.

Loviglio, Joann. "Philadelphia Sidewalk Law Protested." Associated Press, January 18, 1999.

Lundy, Katherine Coleman. *Sidewalks Talk: A Naturalistic Study of Street Kids*. New York: Garland, 1995.

Marcuse, P. "Neutralizing Homelessness." *Socialist Review* 18 (1988): 69–96.

Myers, Patricia. "The Circus Is His Life; Aerialist Is 6th-Generation Performer." *Arizona Republic/Phoenix Gazette*, December 27, 1996.

Nissen, Hans J. *The Early History of the Ancient Near East, 9000–2000 B.C.* Chicago: University of Chicago Press, 1988.

Parish, Steven M. *Hierarchy and Its Discontents: Culture and the Politics of Consciousness in Caste Society*. Philadelphia: University of Pennsylvania Press, 1996.

Price, Jenny. "At Least 4 Dead in School Shooting." Associated Press, March 14, 1998.

Reavis, Dick J. *The Ashes of Waco: An Investigation*. Syracuse: Syracuse University Press, 1995.

Ribeiro, Darcy. *The Civilizational Process*. Washington, D.C.: Smithsonian Institution Press, 1968.

Rivera, Barbara. "Circus Life a Family Affair." *Tulsa World,* April 22, 1998.

Sabloff, Jeremy A. "Maya." *Encyclopedia Americana—International Edition.* Danbury, Conn.: Grolier, 1992.

Shiner, Michael, and Tim Newburn. "Definitely, Maybe Not? The Normalization of Recreational Drug Use Amongst Young People." *Journal of the British Sociological Association* 31, 3 (August 1997): 511–529.

Suro, Roberto. "Other Drugs Supplanting Cocaine Use; Methaphetamine, Heroin on the Rise, White House Reports." *Washington Post,* June 25, 1997.

Times Books. *Past Worlds: The Times Atlas of Archaeology.* Maplewood, N.J.: Hammond, 1988.

Toth, Jennifer. *The Mole People: Life in the Tunnels Beneath New York City.* Chicago: Chicago Review Press, 1993.

Wagner, David. *Checkerboard Square: Culture and Resistance in a Homeless Community.* Boulder: Westview Press, 1993.

Worden, Amy. "Amish Arrested in Gang Drug Bust." Associated Press, June 23, 1998.

Wright, Talmadge. *Out of Place: Homeless Mobilizations, Subcities, and Contested Landscapes.* Albany: State University of New York Press, 1997.

Zuckoff, Mitchell. "Under the Little Top; Welcome to the Big Apple Circus, Where a Community of Performers Juggles Life's Ups and Downs in a Single Magical Ring." *Boston Globe,* July 5, 1992.

Thematic Index

Nearly all the themes of *Beyond Civilization* have been explored in earlier works. This index was designed to aid in tracing their development through time. Numbers immediately following index entries refer to this volume. Page numbers for *Ishmael* (ISH), *The Story of B* (TSOB), and *My Ishmael* (MI) refer to the trade paperback editions of these books, published by Bantam Books.

Dial-a-tribe

The New Tribal Revolution is nothing if not a great *educational* experiment, and it can only succeed if we share our wisdom, experiences, and discoveries with regard to making a living tribally. Luckily, we have a terrific medium for doing exactly this by way of the internet. At www.newtribalventures.com you can be in touch with like–minded readers ready for involvement in this next great adventure.

Those who are not online can reach me at Beyond Civilization, P.O. Box 66627, Houston TX 77266–6627. Your letters are gratefully received and will always be read with interest, but please understand that I can't answer each one individually.